THE
REDBOOK
REPORT
ON
FEMALE
SEXUALITY

THE REDBOOK REPORT ON FEMALE SEXUALITY

100,000 Married Women Disclose the Good News About Sex

Carol Tavris
and
Susan Sadd

DELACORTE PRESS/NEW YORK

Published by
Delacorte Press
1 Dag Hammarskjold Plaza
New York, New York 10017

Library of Congress Cataloging in Publication Data

Tavris, Carol.
The Redbook report on female sexuality.

Bibliography: p.
Includes index.
1. Women—United States—Sexual behavior.
2. Sex in marriage. 3. Married women—United
States. I. Sadd, Susan, joint author. II. Title.
HO29.T38   301.41′8′0655   77–24616

ISBN 0–440–07560–2

ACKNOWLEDGMENTS

Grateful acknowledgment is made for permission to use the following material.

Column by Neil Solomon: Copyright © 1976, Los Angeles Times. Reprinted with permission.

Chart on page 30 by Eugene E. Levitt and Albert D. Klassen, Jr.: From "Public Attitudes Toward Sexual Behaviors: The Latest Investigation of the Institute for Sex Research." Paper presented at the Annual Convention, American Orthopsychiatric Association, New York, New York, June 1973. Table 2.

Chart on page 37 from SEXUAL BEHAVIOR IN THE 1970'S by Morton Hunt: Copyright © 1974 by Playboy Press. Used by permission.

"The Lovemaking: His and Hers" by Eve Merriam: from THE DOUBLE BED by Eve Merriam. Copyright © 1958, 1972 by Eve Merriam. Reprinted by permission of the publishers, M. Evans and Company, Inc., New York, New York 10017 and Eve Merriam c/o International Creative Management.

"I Hear America Swinging" by Peter De Vries: Copyright © 1974, 1976 by Peter De Vries. From I HEAR AMERICA SWINGING by Peter De Vries by permission of Little, Brown and Co. and A. Watkins, Inc.

"The elephant is slow to mate . . ." by D. H. Lawrence: Used by permission of Laurence Pollinger Ltd., William Heinemann Ltd. and the Estate of Mrs. Frieda Lawrence.

Questionnaire on pages 148–149: From "The Experience of Orgasm: His and Hers" by Linda Rosen., ADVISOR Magazine, April 1977. Copyright © 1977 Playgirl Advisor, Inc. Used by permission of Linda Rosen and Playgirl.

Excerpts from IS SEX NECESSARY? by James Thurber and E. B. White: Copyright © 1929, 1957 James Thurber and E. B. White. From IS SEX NECESSARY?, published by Harper & Row, Publishers, New York. Used by permission of Mrs. James Thurber. Copyright © 1947 by James Thurber and E. B. White, Hamish Hamilton Ltd., London.

08961

In Memory of Robert J. Levin

CONTENTS

ACKNOWLEDGMENTS   *xi*

PREFACE *by Sey Chassler*   *xiii*

1. OF SURVEYS AND SEX ɪɴ ᴛʜᴇ Mᴇʟᴏɴ   *1*
The Privacy Paradox   *4*
Measuring Drive and Desire   Cᴏʟᴏɴʏ   *10*
   Talkers and Prudes: The Volunteer Question   *12*
   Breadth versus Depth   *15*
Ah, Sweet Mystery of Life . . .   *23*

2. PREMARITAL SEX   *27*
The Decline and Fall of the American Virgin   *32*
The Effect of Church and School   *38*
Not Whether, but When: Age at Initiation   *43*
   The Precocious Fifteens   *46*
   The Promiscuity Question   *47*
Pleasure, Passion, and the Big O   *50*
Premarital Now, Adultery Later?   *54*
The Pill and the Modern Teenager   *56*
A Summary of the Premarital Scene: Old News and New
   News   *59*

3. MARITAL SEX   *60*
A Digression: Two Women   *65*

Ingredients of Good Sex, Part I: What Happens in Bed

Quality versus Quantity   66
Age and Eroticism   70
Orgasm and Arousal   73
The Active/Passive Dimension: Who Takes the Lead?   80
Variety, the Spice of Sex   83
   Oral-genital Sex   86
   Anal Sex   90
Masturbation   94

Ingredients of Good Sex, Part II: It's All in Your Mind

   Religion and Satisfaction   97
   Communication   106

4. EXTRAMARITAL SEX   111
Extramarital Sex: Who, What, Where, When . . .   114
Extramarital Sex: . . . and Why   120
The 6-Percent Solution   129
Swingers and Swappers   134
A Summary of the Extramarital Scene   137
Old News and New News   142

5. THE GOOD NEWS ABOUT MEN *by Carol Tavris*   143

APPENDIX: Questionnaire and Responses   159

BIBLIOGRAPHY   171

INDEX   179

ACKNOWLEDGMENTS

We would like to express our thanks and appreciation to the people who made this book possible: especially Sey Chassler, Editor-in-Chief of *Redbook,* for his commitment to the survey and his belief in its importance, and Betty Kelly, our editor at Delacorte, whose unflappable enthusiasm for the book and its subject kept us going. We also thank Helene Pleasants and Catherine Caldwell Brown for their valuable editorial revisions, and Toby Epstein Jayaratne, who assisted in the early computer work and analysis.

Finally, our love and gratitude to Amy Levin and to the memory of her husband, Bob, both for their work on this project and for the example they provided that inspired it.

—CAROL TAVRIS
SUSAN SADD

PREFACE

Robert J. Levin initiated this book. Before he died, in May 1976, he had been for many years the Articles Editor of *Redbook* magazine. During those years he brought to fruition his intense and devoted desire to help people to find ways of understanding themselves. Since sex is such a pervasive and intrinsic part of our lives, Bob had always felt that if one could but understand one's sexual self, one could understand—and appreciate—one's total self.

In 1974 he wrote a book about sex with William H. Masters and Virginia E. Johnson, the pioneering sex researchers and co-directors of the Reproductive Biology Research Foundation. It was called *The Pleasure Bond,* a title originated by his wife, Amy, and deeply indicative of Bob's own attitude toward sex. In his preface to *The Pleasure Bond,* he wrote:

"... There are three elements that contribute to sexual functioning—knowledge, comfort and choice—and they are interlocking, mutually reinforcing elements. *To know* is one thing, *to be comfortable* with what one knows is another; *to choose* what is right for oneself is still another."

This single sentence seems to me to outline not only Bob's personal and professional goal but also the goal which he had brought to the beginnings of the book you are about to read. This book, *The Redbook Report on Female Sexuality*, was originally to have been written by Bob. He had just begun it when his life ended.

The book began as a project in *Redbook*. In October 1974, the magazine published a questionnaire called "How Do You Really Feel About Sex?" We received more than 100,000 replies to the questions, which were extremely intimate and probing. This response to a questionnaire was unprecedented in magazine history, and has not been equaled since. The replies produced a body of information about sexual attitudes of women that is extremely valuable.

The questions were designed by Robert R. Bell, a Temple University sociologist, who used them for surveys in the United States and Australia. When we first saw Bell's questionnaire we pondered a good deal the question of whether it was suitable for publication in a magazine read by ten million women. We asked ourselves if it was too frank or too provocative or in bad taste, but we came back repeatedly to Bob Levin's search for some basic truths about people and to his desire to help people *to know, to be comfortable,* to be able *to choose* what is right for oneself. And so we made the decision to publish the questionnaire. Bob and Amy Levin collaborated on the survey itself and on the articles reporting on it in *Redbook* in September and October 1975.

I think it is important to know these things about this book because genesis is often as important as conclusions. Bob and I and all of the editors of *Redbook* have been, and continue to be, vitally interested in what women are thinking, where they are going, where they want to go, and how tradition, convention, and the ways of the world impinge upon these matters. This interest produced *The Redbook Report,* and the interest of modern women in themselves produced its conclusions. Modern women. It is doubtful that these questions could have been asked, much less published and answered, at any other time in recent history, and it is a tribute to the renaissance of the women's movement that modern women feel free to discuss themselves so fully.

When it was no longer possible for this book to be written by Bob Levin, we had to find a new author for it, someone who shared his views and ours, someone who knew the subject matter and was as sensitive to the human potential (as well as the human dilemma) as Bob was. His friend and our colleague Carol Tavris agreed to write the book for us. As a writer with a Ph.D. in social psychology, she was perfectly suited to the task. She has written articles for *Redbook, Ms., Psychology Today,* and *New York*, and is coauthor of a textbook on sex differences, *The Longest War*. She chose as her collaborator Susan Sadd, who has a Ph.D. in social psychology and has worked with *Redbook* on other surveys. They are a remarkably synchronized partnership. This, then, is not Bob Levin's book; it is Carol and Susan's book—but he would have liked it and honored it.

Looking back over these pages, I find that I have written much about the past and little about what you will find here. What will you find? You will find an invigorating sense of life, a churning and bubbling of ideas, a source book for information about the lives of women and, if you are a woman, about your own life. You will find a sense of joy and a sense of fun, a sense of comfort and a sense of play. Out of the statistics Carol Tavris and Susan Sadd have produced a happy, solid book, something good to read and absorb. This is in a sense a book of science, yet it is not essentially a book of conclusions. Rather, it is a genesis. A book of beginnings. Begin, then.

SEY CHASSLER
Editor-in-Chief
Redbook

THE
REDBOOK
REPORT
ON
FEMALE
SEXUALITY

1

OF SURVEYS AND SEX

Licence my roaving hands, and let them go,
Behind, before, above, between, below.
O my America! my new-found-land,
My kingdome, safeliest when with one man man'd,
My Myne of precious stones: My Emperie,
How blest am I in this discovering thee!
To enter in these bonds, is to be free;
Then where my hand is set, my seal shall be.
  Full nakedness! All joyes are due to thee,
As souls unbodied, bodies uncloth'd must be,
To taste whole joyes. Jems which you women use
Are like Atlanta's balls, cast in mens views,
That when a fools eye lighteth on a Jem,
His earthly soul may covet theirs, not them:
Like pictures or like books gay coverings made
For lay-men, are all women thus array'd.
Themselves are mystick books, which only we
(Whom their imputed grace will dignifie)
Must see reveal'd. Then since that I may know;
As liberally, as to a Midwife shew
Thy self: cast all, yea, this white lynnen hence,
There is no pennance due to innocence:
  To teach thee I am naked first; why than
What needst thou have more covering then a man?
                            —JOHN DONNE
                            "Elegie: Going to Bed"

Sex is by no means everything. It varies, as a matter of fact, from only as high as 78 per cent of everything to as low as 3.10 per cent. The norm, in a sane, healthy person, should be between 18 and 24 per cent. In these hectic days, however, it is not unusual to hear even intelligent persons say, or imply, that sex is everything. This, of course, leads to the mistaken idea that a couple who are, so to speak, emotionally compatible are going to be compatible in every other way. "Take care of sex, and the details will look after themselves," is the rule. Nothing could be more stupid. A man and woman may be very, very happy emotionally and not get anywhere at all.

> —JAMES THURBER and E. B. WHITE,
> *Is Sex Necessary?*

Almost fifty years ago, Thurber and White wrote a cheerful spoof of sex research because they were persuaded that "doctors, psychiatrists and other students of misbehavior were pursuing sex to the last ditch, and the human animal seemed absorbed in self-analysis. The heavy writers had got sex down and were breaking its arm." The situation has not improved since their day. On the contrary, the last two decades have produced an unabashed florescence of studies and surveys about sex. The social pendulum has swung from silence about sex to obsession with it. In the fallout from the sexual explosion, some people lost their lovers, many people lost their tempers, and most people lost their senses of humor.

One unintended consequence of all the talk about sexual techniques and mechanics is that people now tend to speak about sex as if it were an individual hobby, like stamp collecting, and about love affairs as if they were encounters between two alien sexual forces—his and hers. These days we hear more about the problems of sex than about its pleasures. Books teach and preach how to do it, how often to do it, whether to do it; a few people are saying the hell with all of it. One disgruntled woman wrote to *Redbook*: "All this sex business has turned me off. Believe it or not I can get along very well without it, because I've found other emotional outlets which are more fun and don't numb my senses. You ought to try it some time." Unfortunately, she did not specify what alternative she was recommending.

The reason for this book, which after all is about another sex survey, is that it is time for some good news. It is time to hear from women who are not swingers, swappers, or equestriennes on the sexual carousel. *Redbook* magazine gave its middle American readers a chance to speak up: In its October 1974 issue *Redbook* published a questionnaire on a range of sexual experiences and invited women to reply. They replied in droves, bunches, and bevies: More than 100,000 women sent back the questionnaire, a number unprecedented in sex research. These women are especially interesting because in their religious and political beliefs they approximate the national profile, whereas most sex surveys draw disproportionate numbers of people who are nonreligious and politically liberal. Hundreds of *Redbook* readers sent in letters along with their answers, and many more wrote to share their reactions when the magazine published its early findings in 1975.

These 100,000 women, whatever their age, education, and religion, are having a merry time. Most of them like their husbands, their marriages, and their sex lives. They are active partners; they do not close their eyes, grit their teeth, and do their duty, as Victorian mothers advised. Their sexual pleasures do not fade with familiarity, either: They enjoy sex with their husbands no matter how long they have been married. Their responses to the survey celebrate love, marriage, and undisguised lust. The rich mine of information they provided shows some important trends in the sex life of the American wife. Some highlights:

• The stronger a woman's religious beliefs, the more she is likely to feel satisfied with her sex life.

• Premarital sex has little effect on sex in marriage; it doesn't improve marital sex *or* make it worse. Women who have had sex before marriage are as likely as those who were virgins at marriage to be happily married, to experiment sexually in marriage, to enjoy sex and have it often.

• Promiscuity is not increasing among young women. Although the great majority do have sex before marriage, it is with the man they love and plan to marry. Young wives are not more apt than older wives to have fooled around with lots of lovers before marriage.

• Fifteen is a watershed year for first sexual intercourse. Regardless of their current age, women whose sexual initiation occurred by age fifteen differ from those who waited even one year longer before having sex. The precocious fifteens are more likely to have many sexual partners before marriage, to have extramarital sex after marriage, to be more sexually experimental and active, and to be less happy in general and in their marriages.

• Almost all wives under the age of forty enjoy oral-genital sex, both cunnilingus and fellatio.

• Almost half of these women have tried anal intercourse, though much less frequently than oral sex. Their attitude is "with love, anything goes," and the more sexually uninhibited a wife is, the happier she is with her sex life.

• So far as young women are concerned, sex should come not only out of the closet, but also out of the bedroom. They no longer believe that sex requires specific times, places, and positions, and they are trying sex in all its variations and combinations.

• The more openly a wife can discuss her sexual feelings and preferences with her husband, the happier she is—with her sex life, her marriage, and herself. Wives who think sex is something to be done, not discussed, are less satisfied.

• Many women enjoy happy, healthy sex lives throughout their sixties and seventies, and even later. All it takes is the right attitude and a willing partner.

• Extramarital sex still typically reflects problems in a marriage, but almost 30 percent of the wives who responded to this questionnaire have had an extramarital affair, and a substantial number of them combine outside love affairs with a happy marriage.

THE PRIVACY PARADOX

In the olden days, when no one knew what anyone else was doing sexually, a woman might worry that something was wrong with her if she did not simply endure sex but actually wanted it. If you were a bawdy wife in 1865 who liked your sexual pleasures, you would have been depressed to read the most popular sex-advice book of the day, Dr. William Acton's *Functions and Disorders of the Reproductive Organs*. Dr. Acton was happy to tell you whatever you wanted to know, even if he didn't know it himself. He blithely asserted, for example, that "the majority of women (happily for them) are not very much troubled with sexual feelings of any kind. What men are habitually, women are only exceptionally." A proper wife and mother would squelch any murmur of a tingle of a titillation, while a man, poor lecherous thing, was known to need occasional sexual release.

Today we know that women have the same sexual feelings as men. The announcement has been sounded so insistently on the media drums, however, that a new set of worries has been created. Now some people fret if they or their partners don't want sex at all hours of the day and night. "Sometimes I'm simply too involved in my work or a personal project to get overly interested in sex," one woman wrote. "So what do I get from my husband? 'What's the matter with you? You must be frigid or something!' Thank you for allowing me to express myself."

Sex is the most private of expressions, and, unlike other activities, it does not offer standards for comparison. In most realms of behavior people can compare themselves to others and get a pretty good idea of how they are doing; a person *knows* if she is clumsy at ice-skating or graceful at water polo. Grades, promotions, income, praise—all are tangible signs of success at work. But there are no grades (thank God) for sexual performance. No rules. No classes for beginners, intermediates, and experts. As a result, many people muddle along in a middle range between their desires and doubts, knowing what they want to do and wondering whether they should.

Under such conditions of uncertainty, people rely on surveys for reassurance that they are "normal." But information about sex reassures some and inhibits others, a dilemma perfectly summed up in one letter: "I am tired of hearing about sex, reading about it, etc. All it does is make you wonder—gee, am I weird because I am not doing weird sexual things? I am glad, though, that there is candor. It has enabled my husband and me to discuss our individual sexuality with less inhibition. And I can look on my early feelings about sex and love with less guilt."

We were startled to find how many women, in this supposedly open era, looked to the questionnaire findings for permission to be truly sexual. They were longing for the safety of numbers to assure them that they could do what they wanted to without fearing that they were "sick." "I waited with large amounts of anxiety to see what your results would be," wrote a wife married thirteen years. "I was really amazed to read that there are so many women just like myself. It's really a great relief to know that I am not alone. My strongest desires for sexual pleasure are finally liberated. All my inhibition toward different types of sexual pleasure are gone for good. I was actually embarrassed to answer the questionnaire, but I did with complete honesty. I am so relieved to see that so many women have my own desires, and to read that oral-genital sex is a natural source of physical and emotional gratification."

A twenty-six-year-old mother of three added: "I've always considered myself a sexually liberated woman, but some of the questions on your survey were embarrassing for me. I wasn't quite so sure of my normality. Your report has put to rest all my fears, as well as the fears of thousands of other 'sexually liberated' women, I'm sure. You see, no matter how open and free we profess to be about sex, I think most of us are still strongly inhibited by society's influence on what a 'good girl' may and may not do sexually. Now it's so nice to know we can admit it because we are normal—not naughty!"

But the survey made some women feel abnormal, part of a besieged minority. One wife, hoping that the survey would tell her that she had "a *normally* rotten relationship," was disappointed to read that so many of the 100,000 respondents had happier marriages. Another explained that she had never liked cunnilingus; that she thinks it is dirty and unpleasant; that after many fights her husband had agreed to accept her feelings. "My husband read your article [on the results of the survey]," she wrote wistfully, "and now he thinks I'm an oddball because I don't like oral sex when the majority of women do. You brought more trouble into our marriage."

Such readers regarded the survey as a bully, instructing people on what they must do to be "normal." "I got the definite impression," wrote an angry reader, "that your magazine was inviting all women to stop being square and start living it up with more affairs and more excitement in their life—I was disgusted!" Several were concerned that too much information about sex condones immorality: "For people who have wishbones instead of backbones, to read of thousands of women doing such things [as having premarital and extramarital sex] puts a stamp of approval on them and would lead many to follow suit." Presumably she was a person of backbone.

Apparently the need to feel that one's own sex life is normal is so strong, and the thought of being deviant is so abhorrent, that many people find it hard to regard sex studies with detachment. If the study confirms one's prejudices, it is a model of truth and perspicacity. If it jars with one's experiences, it is a monument of lies and stupidities. When the magazine report was published, women with good sex lives wrote to sing its praises. "It is such a relief to know that someone cares about how a woman feels about sex," wrote one. "Not how she is supposed to feel but how she really lives with it." But women with unhappy sex lives think that most women "really" live in misery, and they dismissed the optimistic results as the distorted rantings of "sex weirdos" and "nymphomaniacs." "These polls are not representative of the present-day female," wrote a forty-nine-year-old nurse. "I do not think you can ever get a true picture of the sexual happiness of people. Men are prone to exaggerate and women are ashamed to tell the truth." The truth, as she saw it, was that most women are sexually dissatisfied and that the *Redbook* respondents undoubtedly were "egotistical women who felt the need to reinforce their sexual frustrations by lying." She did not explain why she was one of the few who felt obliged to admit the truth.

Several men, too, judged the survey not by its results but by the yardstick of their own marriages. If their wives do not enjoy sex, then no one else's does, either. The news that a great majority of the 100,000 respondents are sexually active, like to take the sexual initiative, and have orgasms would obviously be depressing to a husband who feels sexually deprived. "I think most of the women lied," wrote one such man. "Most men would be more than pleased if their wives would have 'willing' sex once a week—and would consider themselves fortunate indeed to have sex twice a month!" In his experience, he went on, men *never* have sex frequently enough, *never* have partners who enjoy sex, and *never* have wives who anticipate sex with pleasure (emphasis his). Another husband sent along a home-designed questionnaire for men, asking what their wives "let" them do sexually ("Does your wife let you kiss her breasts?" "How often does she let you touch her?"). He attributed all of his ills and ailments, including his chain smoking, to the fact that his wife wouldn't "let him" do anything.

Letters like his make a person yearn to fix up deprived husbands with deprived wives. One woman wrote to say how relieved she was to find out that she was healthy after all, "with the same attitudes on sexuality as most others who responded." She had been afraid that something was wrong with her because she wanted sex more often than her husband did; he wanted it four to six times a year. A Texas wife used the survey to try to convince her husband that women do enjoy sex. She was unsuccessful. "He doesn't believe that a woman needs to be satisfied as far as sex. He says that 85 percent of women are never satisfied and accept it, and let their husbands use them. I don't believe this at all. I asked him to see a doctor but he laughed and said I was the one that needed a doctor. I know as a woman that sex should last more than a few seconds."

The stories of such deadlocks can break your heart, and they are the real answer to those who wonder whether sex research is necessary. How prevalent are couples like the Texas wife and her husband, or the chain-smoking husband and his unresponsive wife? When most people try to imagine the national sexual landscape, they extrapolate not only from their own experience but from their perceptions of their friends and neighbors—who are more like them, of course, than they realize. Many of the letters that came in, on whatever topic, began "My friends and I think ..." or ended "... and my friends agree with me." Happy couples think the whole world is in love, as this letter from a conservative housewife in Portage, Pennsylvania, shows:

> It is still possible to find couples who are faithful to each other and find happiness and freedom in love and trust. My husband and I have found a very happy fulfilling life in love and sex for thirty-two years without premarital sex or extramarital sex. Most of the people with whom I associate have equally happy marriages.

But unhappy couples think everyone suffers. We quote from one housewife's letter at length because it stands in such contrast to the survey's good news, because it could have been written one hundred years ago, because it represents a portrait of female sexuality that many think is still the norm:

> Before I got married, I was like all other women, panting to experience the ecstasy of sex. I had read and heard (from men) the wonder of it. Well, I married a wonderful man and we have been married almost 30 years. From the first night it was just unpleasant, I endured it, but I have always resented my husband's flight to the heights while I experience "blah." Thank goodness the last three years he has slowed down so I don't have to act the part of enjoying something so repulsive. I really love my husband but he is a man and to him sex is food.
>
> Now what I want to tell you is I am not alone in this. In all of my life I have *never* talked to a woman who did not feel as I do. Not once have I heard a woman say she enjoys sex. I hear them call it repulsive, tell the things they do to get out of it (sitting up late to avoid it, stealing into bed without waking their husbands). They shudder at the thought of this going on into their sixties, seventies.
>
> Okay, who is kidding whom?
>
> P.S. I think this women's liberation is silly mostly, but I'm all for the part that says we can stop faking orgasms.

The mischievous demons that invented sex created a devious paradox. Ignorance confers many blessings, not the least of which is the security of one's superstitions. Ignorance allows people to assume that everyone else is in the same boat. Information reassures people whose sex lives are already good, but it worries the deprived. As Faust learned, knowledge has a price.

So long as there are women and men who endure sex and consider it repulsive, a duty like washing socks, the benefits of sexual studies will far outweigh the costs. Information about the great range of sexual behavior that is normal and fun is worth the time of uncertainty as people search for the sexual code that fits them comfortably. In the best of all possible worlds, people would not use surveys to tell them that what they want to do is all right, or that they must do what they have no desire for. They would know enough about sex and about themselves to make wise choices, and they would regard new studies as illuminations of the behavior of their fellow creatures. In that golden future, more people might be secure in the blessings of privacy, and answer questionnaires the way this woman did:

> I liked it better when how many times and what I did with my husband or loved man remained in my bedroom as well as my heart and memory. Frankly, after digesting your survey, and feeling a little bit horny and quite a bit cut up, I wanted nothing more but to go and see a nice innocuous Walt Disney movie.

MEASURING DRIVE AND DESIRE

> I do not think your report gives the right impression. After all, you are only reporting on the women who sent in your questionnaire. What about all the others? The majority of women who sent it in naturally would be the women with low morals. Here in Oklahoma City, the ladies are not near as evil as you would like us to believe. But you want to make it appear all women are falling apart.

> I decided to answer your questionnaire because I felt that the only people who return sexual questionnaires are the ones who wish to shock and therefore answer with weird answers and those which may make their own sexual fantasies seem not so abnormal. I am really happy and pleased with my husband and lover even after 30 years.

In the sex business, you can't please most of the people any of the time. Half of the people in the world want to hear good news about sex and the rest want to hear bad news, and neither side agrees on which is what. Sexual revolutionaries look for evidence that total liberation is around the corner, that people are jumping in and out of beds like fleas. Conservatives use the same evidence to worry about moral decay and the fall of Rome.

> I am bewildered by attempts of proponents of both moralities to shove their moral standards down my throat.

I am sick of being told that I am a prude if I do not jump on the bandwagon because "everybody else is doing it." I am also sick of the old-morality people telling me that the society is morally decadent because not everyone in it accepts their particular moral standards. I think that both sides have gone off the deep end in their zeal to promote their brand of morality.

The problem lies partly in the nature of the data, in the fact that all sex surveys are biased to some extent. Researchers often joke that there are two kinds of people who do not answer sex questionnaires: those who are perfectly happy and those who are perfectly miserable. The first group cannot understand why anyone would have problems with an activity that is so simple and jolly. They don't answer surveys because it does not occur to them why they should. Researchers are delighted by the comments of these people, who typically react to their work by saying, "How lovely that you are doing all this research, but is it really necessary?"*

In contrast are the people who do not respond because they find the subject of sex disgusting, embarrassing, shocking, or immoral. Many of their letters include the catch phrase "I'm no prude, but . . .":

I think the people answering your survey (not all) were sex weirdos and oversexed women. I am not a prude because a lot of my friends feel the same way about your article.

It is disgraceful the way Sex is being exploited in this late stage. It has been around since Adam and Eve but one would think it was just discovered. It is literature like that [that] causes rape and crime today.
P.S. *And I am not a prude!*

---

*These folks know what they need to about sex, even when ignorance is bliss. Masters and Johnson are fond of telling the old story of the couple who are celebrating their fiftieth wedding anniversary with a big family party. Their son John, a surgeon, is delayed at his hospital and joins the party somewhat late. "I'm so happy you got here, dear," the mother says. "What sort of surgery did you have to do?" There is a lull in the conversation as John answers quietly, "Well, Mother, it had to do with a man's penis." "Oh dear," she replies, "I do hope you didn't have to take the bone out." Whereupon the entire dinner party stands and drinks a toast to her husband.

By compiling such a questionnaire and publishing the results you are helping to lower the morals of the people in our country. I'm sure you will not agree with me and think me a prude.

I'm no prude, but I do believe if you make a commitment you should hold it in every way especially sexually. It makes me happy to see that there are still women who are upholding their marriage vows in this day and time of "anything goes."

Talkers and Prudes: The Volunteer Question

As a result of the self-selection factor in much of sex research (a problem called "volunteer bias"), respondents tend to be younger, better educated, somewhat more liberal, and more affluent than the average American. (We do not know as much about the sex life of prudes, as it is hard to find a prude who will admit to being one.) The direction of bias depends a good deal on the kind of survey and the ease of answering it: Does the person have to go out to meet an interviewer, write away for the questionnaire, fill out some questions at home? Are the questions closed-ended (the respondent picks one of a list of predetermined answers) or open-ended (the respondent answers in his or her own words)? Most researchers have neither the resources nor the public support to select every fourth house in a census tract and march in, clipboards at the ready, asking ninety-seven impertinent questions of everyone in the family. As a result, they must make do with the most accessible people and the best available methods.

During the forties, Alfred Kinsey and his colleagues spent years conducting personal interviews with thousands of individuals. Kinsey, a biologist who studied insects, collected sexual statistics as he had previously collected gall wasps: compulsively, meticulously, indefatigably. He quickly became adept at detecting braggarts and exaggerators, as well as drawing out the shy and uncertain. To get around (somewhat) the problem of volunteer bias, Kinsey often signed up whole groups of his lecture audiences, and many people found themselves seduced into interviews by Kinsey's charm and persuasiveness. His associate, Wardell Pomeroy, recalls:

The interviewing trips were a grand tour through America. From conventional Miami or Philadelphia, we might be plunged into the life of minuscule communities like Nicodemus, Kansas. Suburban matrons would be followed by prostitutes in prisons, highly placed executives by underworld characters. Often, in our explorations, we would plunge into a subculture that was unknown to people not only in the city where it existed, but to 90 percent of the public in general [such as the world of homosexual prostitution]. (page 132)*

Nevertheless, the Kinsey reports on male and female sexuality were not based on a random cross section of the American public. They did not get enough people from certain segments of the population—especially blacks, the poor, the uneducated—and some critics feel they oversampled other segments, notably homosexuals. But Kinsey's group did gather the first systematic, nationwide, detailed data on sexual practices; their research stands as the base line against which subsequent studies of sexual behavior and attitudes have been measured.

Kinsey's books had barely seen the light of day before the critics pounced. Two psychologists, Abraham Maslow and J. M. Sakoda, were especially interested in how Kinsey's volunteers might have differed from those who refused to be interviewed. Maslow appealed to students in his psychology classes who had been approached by Kinsey, explained what he wanted to know, and asked them to fill out an inventory of their sexual attitudes and behavior. All of his students previously had taken a self-esteem test, so Maslow could see whether self-esteem affected a person's willingness to participate in a sex study and whether it affected his or her sex life.

Maslow and Sakoda found that the students who had volunteered for Kinsey's interviews scored significantly higher on the self-esteem scale and were less likely to be virgins than those who did not volunteer. "The bias introduced into a sex study by the use of volunteers," they concluded, "is in general in the direction of inflating the percentage reporting unconventional or disapproved

*For references, see Bibliography.

sexual behavior—such as masturbation, oral sexuality, petting to climax, premarital and extramarital, etc. . . .''

Conservatives would have cheered. They knew all those people couldn't be doing all the dirty things that Kinsey reported.

Since Maslow and Sakoda's study, twenty-five years ago, the topic of volunteer bias in research has become a major field of inquiry in psychology. Generally, it is still true that sexual liberals are more willing to answer sex surveys than sexual conservatives. But the bias may no longer be as serious as it once was. The climate has changed since Kinsey's day, and more people are ready to talk about their sexual feelings and experiences.

For example, in 1973 Karl Bauman did an update on the volunteer issue. He selected 1,000 men and 1,000 women at random from the registrar's list at his university and wrote to them, requesting that they come to a specific location to participate in a survey on sexual attitudes and practices. The number of students who showed up was dismally small: only 150 men and 196 women. Then Bauman drew another random sample of students. This time he went to see them personally to persuade them to fill out the questionnaire, waited while they did the task, and even walked with them to a mailbox to post the survey, to assure them of anonymity. This time everyone agreed to participate. What were the differences between the two groups, the volunteers and the truly randoms? None. Women and men in both samples were alike in their sexual attitudes, experience, use of birth control, permissiveness, number of lovers, and so on. The only difference was that religious men, but not religious women, were reluctant to volunteer for the survey.

Another college study of volunteers and captives, in 1971, got similar results, with one interesting difference. Gilbert Kaats and Keith Davis compared the questionnaires of three groups: students in their classes who were required to fill them out; students who began the questionnaire in class but then were free to finish it at home or not, as they wished; and students who volunteered to take a sex questionnaire instead of doing an alternative project. The researchers found very few differences among the three groups. For example, virgins were as likely to volunteer as nonvirgins were. The only group that stood out was the last: the students who were actively eager to be in a sex study, who went to the *extra effort* of going to a research center to make their opinions known, had the most liberal sexual attitudes and, especially among women, were the most experienced sexually.

Studies like these provide a handle for dealing with the problem of volunteer bias. We can no longer assume reflexively that only liberals, nymphomaniacs, and moral degenerates answer sex surveys. Plenty of conservatives, prudes, and guardians of public morality want to get their two cents' worth in also. The task is to evaluate each survey in terms of the population it draws from, the amount of effort that respondents must expend to participate, and the demographic profile of its participants: Are they all urban New Yorkers who will discuss sex as readily as city blight? Are they rural Kansans who wouldn't talk about sex if it were the last subject left on earth?

Few researchers today have the obsession and sheer stamina to interview thousands of people, as Kinsev did. Most use questionnaires and nab whatever group of willing participants is at hand: college students, neighbors, magazine readers, members of organizations. A few surveys based on representative samples of the American population have been done, but they are few and far between. Even in these landmark studies, though, the problem of volunteer bias is rarely eliminated completely. Morton Hunt's study for the Playboy Foundation, *Sexual Behavior in the 1970's,* used established public-opinion teams in twenty-four cities to administer questionnaires to randomly selected adults. Even so, only one person in five agreed to participate. And that response is considered good.

Because of all the technical problems in sex research, social scientists have to regard each study as part of a mosaic. Each fragment adds something to the understanding of whether and how behavior has changed over the years, who is affected, the direction in which we are headed. When the results of many studies start to converge, we can be sure we are on to something.

Breadth versus Depth

Of course, a major controversy in this field is not just over who volunteers, but what they say. One researcher will prefer to do intensive interviews with a handful of people, in order to describe the subjective side of sex. Another takes the fast-and-snappy questionnaire method, in order to describe the objective experiences of thousands of people. It is not that one method has a firmer handle on truth than the other, simply that each finds different truths. One technique tries to reveal emotions, conflicts, and motives; the other tallies coital acts faster than you can have them. One provides information on the complex nuances of sex without considering the overall scope; the other provides information on the range of behavior at the expense of nuance.

Consider Shere Hite's report on female sexuality, which consists of subjective essays from some 3,000 women. Hite's conclusions differ in many ways from those of the *Redbook* study. Hite says that "most" women do not reach orgasm during intercourse, that masturbation is a more effective route to orgasm than intercourse is, that more women are having homosexual experiences than ever before, that women recognize the extent to which sex is a political act. But most of the 100,000 *Redbook* respondents said that they do indeed reach orgasm during intercourse, that they generally masturbate only when their husbands are away, that they don't prefer masturbation to intercourse, that only a minuscule minority had had a homosexual encounter, and that sex is an act of love, not liberation.

How should a nonprofessional evaluate these two conclusions? By recognizing the strengths and limitations of the survey methods that led to them. Hite says that she was not trying to do a scientific study, but simply letting women speak for themselves about their sex lives. Her book offers a tapestry of provocative experiences, but they are the experiences of a highly select group of women. The reader should regard the book as a collection of personal stories, but the *proportion* of respondents who have Sexual Experience A or Sexual Reaction B cannot be extrapolated to American women in general.

For example, Hite's respondents typically had to write to her for the questionnaire, which was advertised in several magazines. Then they had to spend hours answering the lengthy open-ended questions, each of which consisted of a cluster of queries. Only 3,019 women returned their questionnaires, out of some 100,000 that were mailed out on request. No wonder—a woman would have to be powerfully motivated to tell her sexual history in the minute detail that Hite required, to say nothing of writing away for the questions in the first place. Although the book is subtitled "A Nationwide Study," volunteer bias resulted in a geographical distribution that was rather lopsided: for example, 1 woman from Collbran, Colorado; 1 from Warner Robins, Georgia; 2 from Canoga Park, California; 2 from Akron, Ohio; and 231 from New York City. In sum, Hite's respondents tended to be feminists, unmarried, very liberal sexually, and inclined to view sex as a political act. Indeed, two of the questions were "Do you regard sex in any way as political?" and "Why is [teenage sexuality] presently repressed?"—questions that assume a shared ideology and interpretation of terms. As we noted earlier, studies find that the more trouble a person has to go to in order to contribute a sexual history, the more liberal and sexually active he or she tends to be.

The *Redbook* survey, in contrast, reached a much different audience through a different method. The questionnaire appeared in a magazine that is read by millions of middle American women who are more traditional in their religious and political views. The survey, designed by Dr. Robert Bell of Temple University, consisted of closed-ended questions on a range of sexual experiences and preferences.* Filling out the questionnaire was relatively easy: It was anonymous, it was right there, it required little effort.

But the strength of an objective questionnaire can also be its weakness. The form of the *Redbook* survey meant that data from 100,000 women could be compared and quantified. But all short-answer surveys have to condense a panorama of sensations into a few questions, each offering a limited set of answers. Some women felt frustrated by this format. "I think that any attempt to measure human emotions in terms of statistics is doomed by its very nature to be an exercise in futility," wrote one wife, who nonetheless answered the questions. Another suggested that lust, your basic rousing sex force, can be subjected to scientific scrutiny, while love cannot—the difference, she said, between drive and desire.

In point of fact, though, research has shown that you don't learn much more about a person by giving her open-ended ques-

---

*Bell has used this questionnaire with samples of women in the United States and Australia. (See Appendix for the *Redbook* survey and the distribution of responses.)

tions than by giving her a closed version (if your questions and answers are good). Sometimes people feel better when they can answer in paragraphs instead of by circling answer C, but they don't tell you more about the quality of their lives. We were helped in our search for subjective fleshing out of the numbers, however, by the hundreds of letters that accompanied the questionnaires. They gave color and human dimension to the larger pattern described by the survey.

We recognize what is missing, even so. The *Redbook* survey, like many others, could not capture the dimension of *change*. Most studies freeze the person's experience to one moment in time, and so lose a sense of the highs and lows that occur in all love affairs. They miss the changes of mood and desire that make sex fast and intense on one occasion, leisurely and luxurious on another; the escalation and resolution of conflicts; the times when sex is electric and the times when it is merely comfortable. The assumption is that if the survey reaches enough people, all these wrinkles of variation will be ironed out. But it's the wrinkles, whether on surveys or on faces, that create interest.

Large-scale surveys thus necessarily reduce a woman's experience to averages: "On the average, how long must sexual intercourse last for you to have an orgasm?" This is actually an important question and dates back to Kinsey, who found that a major source of sexual incompatibility between husbands and wives was that men tended to ejaculate quickly (within two minutes of penetration), while women needed at least several minutes of intercourse in order to reach orgasm. Reasonably, one would want to know whether speed of arousal and the ability to reach orgasm are still problems for women. Even so, some women found the question as amusing as we did. "If one is involved in foreplay and sexual intercourse," a respondent asked, "how can one watch the clock?" "Really!" exclaimed another. "I *could* do it in two or three minutes—but why bother? We rarely get done in less than an hour." Another said, "Thirty seconds on some occasions—and 30 minutes on others. How do you average *that?*"

Because of space limitations in the magazine, the questionnaire unfortunately had to omit several questions crucial to female sexuality: notably, whether the wife or the husband uses birth control, what kind, and whether birth control affects their sex life, as many studies have found it does. There was no question about masturbation in childhood and adolescence, but Kinsey and others have shown that masturbation is related to greater sexual responsiveness during intercourse. And there were no questions about whether the women's sexual experiences had gotten better or worse since marriage, or what the women would like to do sexually if they had their druthers.

On balance, however, we think that the questionnaire is important for the picture it provides of a large group of women who usually have neither the opportunity nor the inclination to participate in sex surveys. What the survey lost by being restricted to tightly focused items it gained in the number of people who were able to answer it. By way of comparison, Kinsey et al.'s *Sexual Behavior in the Human Female* was based on interviews with 5,940 women; Hunt's survey consisted of interviews with 100 women and questionnaires from 1,044 more (and about the same numbers of men); Hite got 3,019 replies; a *Psychology Today* readership survey in 1969 drew 20,000 responses. So the 100,000 *Redbook* readers are a unique sample in the annals of sex research.

This is not to say that more numbers always yield better data. As any statistician can tell you, the size of a study has nothing to do with how representative it is. National opinion polls—such as surveys of election preferences and presidential popularity—are based on random samples of all Americans and usually consist of only some 1,200 to 2,000 respondents. That small number, if properly selected, represents the entire population. Every household in the nation has an equal chance of being chosen for the sample, although even the census people admit that minorities may be underrepresented.

The advantage of large numbers in the case of the *Redbook* survey is twofold. First, the sample includes enough women of all educational levels, religious affiliations, ages, occupations, regions, and incomes to permit comparisons across groups. In smaller studies, for example, there are usually not enough respondents with only a grade-school education to enable assessment of the impact of school. But out of 100,000, we could usually draw enough people from groups that surveys often miss. Second, the large size meant that the survey drew a great range of sexual attitudes and experiences, and gave us enough data to be able to say what factors contribute to a happy sex life and a happy marriage. Instead of just describing how many women are doing what, we could determine *which* women were doing what, and why.

Faced with analyzing so many thousands of replies, however, we did what any sane, well-trained researchers would do: we drew a random sample of the 100,000 for computer analysis. The time and cost of processing all of the questionnaires would have been prohibitive, and would not have produced data that were any more reliable; in effect, we created a sample that was as representative of the original 100,000 as the pollster's sample is of the American population. We worked on a basic sample of 2,278 replies and a larger random sample of over 18,000, which we used when we needed more cases for special comparisons.* With considerable reluctance we decided to restrict the study to married and remarried women only. We omitted the small percentage of single women, divorcees, and widows who returned the questionnaire, because we could not say with any confidence that they represented many women in their marital categories.

We do not pretend that the *Redbook* sample represents all American wives, but we can say with confidence that the findings apply to a large group of them, not just to an urban, sexually sophisticated segment of the country. By comparing the profile of respondents to that of married women in general, one can see where *Redbook* readers differ from, or agree with, the national average (see Table 1). They are virtually parallel to the national distribution in geographical area, religious belief, and the percentage who work. But they share the biases of most magazine readers: they are younger, better educated, and more affluent than the average American.

To put the *Redbook* results into context, throughout this report we have drawn on other research to help determine the strength of the findings. For example, when we discuss the number of *Redbook* respondents who have had premarital sex, we also indicate what other studies have found. We were consistently impressed at the strength of our results, which were rarely far out

*Note to researchers: all correlations and statistics reported throughout this text are highly significant, unless otherwise indicated, and have been tested where possible for strength of association as well.

TABLE 1.
REPRESENTATIVENESS OF REDBOOK RESPONDENTS

Geographic area	Redbook (1974)	National (1974)
New England	9%	6%
Mid-Atlantic	19	17
North Central	25	30
South Atlantic	10	14
South Central	15	13
Mountain	4	5
Pacific	15	12
Outside Cont- inental U.S.	4	3
Age		
Under 25	25	21
25–34	52	26
35 and over	23	53
Religion[a]		
Protestant	57	58
Catholic	27	27
Jewish	3	4
Agnostic	6	5 ("No religion")
Other	7	6

Political views[b]	Redbook (1974)	*National* (1974)
Very liberal	4	2
Liberal	23	13
Moderate	57	44
Conservative	15	31
Very conservative	2	

Education[c]		
Grade school	1	21
High-school graduate	37	57
Some college	38	12
College graduate—Advanced degree	13	11

Employment		
Full-time	32	35
Part-time	17	11
Not employed	51	54

Family income[c]		
Less than $5,000	2	11
$5,000–$9,999	18	22
$10,000–$14,999	36	24
$15,000–$24,999	33	28
$25,000 or more	12	12

Number of children[d]	Redbook (1974)	*National* (1974)
0	21	21
1	23	25
2	30	33
3	15	15
4 or more	11	7

[a]National data from Gallup polls, taken in 1973, of adults over age 18.

[b]National data from Harris poll, taken November 1974. An additional 10 percent said "not sure."

[c]U.S. Bureau of the Census, Current Population Reports, 1974, figures for white females (education) and white families (income).

[d]The closest national comparison we could find for this sample of white married women in intact homes lists number of children for husbands (wife present) in the approximate age category of the respondents. U.S. Bureau of the Census, 1974.

Note: In this table, as in others throughout the book, percentages may not total 100 because of rounding to the nearest whole number.

---

of line with the pace and direction of sexual change that other research has documented. The *Redbook* report adds a good chunk to the national mosaic.

AH, SWEET MYSTERY OF LIFE . . .

One clear theme throughout all the letters and statistics that poured in was that sexual happiness is less a matter of mechanics than of communication. Oddly, in spite of, or maybe because of, all the talk about sex in the last decade, it is as difficult as ever for people to express their real desires to the person closest to them. Many find it easier to talk to an impersonal questionnaire than to the familiar stranger in their bedroom.

> Sex is the ultimate means of communication between mar-
> riage partners, and I only wish that a few years ago I could
> have expressed my needs and fears clearly to my husband.
> My self-confidence and feelings toward sex were reinforced
> by your statistics.

To avoid the profound awkwardness caused by sexual vulnerability, many people would sooner suffer in silence than struggle
through a suggestion: "Er, John, would you . . . ah . . . ?" Or they
create elaborate verbal smoke screens to disguise their real problems and fears: "Look, Mary, the reason I couldn't . . . well, you
know . . . is that, er, I was traumatized when I was ten, and, well,
I can only do it with girls I don't like, on the third date, and only
for five minutes at that . . ."

Leonore Tiefer, a sex researcher and therapist, observes that
"because our egos are so excruciatingly vulnerable to criticism
about our sexual abilities, sex is often shrouded in a romantic haze
which is supposed to substitute for communication. I have heard
many women say, 'Well, if he really loved me, he would know
what I want,' and men say, 'If she really loved me, she would be
happy when I make love to her.' They come to therapy expecting
that an expert will tell them a few simple and exotic techniques
that will solve everything." If only it were that simple. The trick
is to learn not only to express one's own needs, but to listen to
one's partner without feeling criticized or unloved.

When all is said and done, a major value of surveys such as
this one is that they provoke dialogue. Sometimes the confidence born of knowing that one is not alone, not sexually deviant, starts the conversation. One wife wrote that she loved her
husband and did not want to leave him, but she was unhappy
about their sex life:

> He is an old-fashioned, once-a-week man. This is enough
> for him but not for me. I'm going to wait to see how
> other women feel about frequency, and if they agree with
> me I'm going to make him read the report. Thank you for
> giving me the chance to sound off on this matter. Maybe
> it will give me the courage to start a very personal discus-
> sion with my husband.

Another wife said that she and her husband had gone over every question together, which "gave us a more open feeling about our relationship. Thank you for bringing those feelings to the surface." Others said that candid discussions with their husbands about their answers—especially on premarital and extramarital sex—caused a few storms, which subsided to the benefit of both partners. But the conversations have begun. One woman, after writing us her lengthy sex history, ended: "In my mother's era I would be writing to share my bread recipe with you. Hurrah for you—and for us!—that we can write of the stuff of life rather than the staff."

We are not far removed from her mother's era, when sex was believed to be a mysterious, mystical happening that revealed itself on its own clumsy schedule. This view effectively kept couples from saying what they meant and meaning what they said, assuming they knew what they meant. The *Redbook* survey may be a harbinger of better relations between the sexes, but it is going to take several generations before men and women truly know how to talk to one another about sex. At that point, people won't confuse the pains of ignorance with the delights of mystery. No one knew the difference better than Thurber and White, as they wrote in "The Lilies and Bluebird Delusion" in *Is Sex Necessary?*:

I have in mind the case of a young lady whose silly mother had taught her to believe that she would have a little son, three years old, named Ronald, as soon as her husband brought a pair of bluebirds into a room filled with lilies-of-the-valley. . . .

When the couple were married, the young husband entered their hotel suite to find it literally a garden of lilies-of-the-valley. He was profoundly touched, but baffled, and asked his wife who was dead.

"Where are the bluebirds?" she replied, coyly.

"What bluebirds?" he demanded.

"The bluebirds," she said, blushing. Unfortunately, but not unnaturally, the bridegroom did not know what the bride was talking about. . . .

"Aren't you going to get any bluebirds?" she persisted.

"I don't know where the hell I'd get any bluebirds to-night," he said, rather irritably, "me not being Bo-Peep."

The nuclear complex was made right then and there. There was a long tense silence, after which the bride burst into tears.

"Now, dear," said her husband, more reasonably, "let's try to get this thing straightened out. What are you talking about, anyway?"

"Sex—if you want to know!" she blurted out, and swooned.

2
PREMARITAL SEX

Amyntas led me to a Grove,
  Where all the Trees did shade us;
The Sun it self, though it had Strove,
  It could not have betray'd us:
The place secur'd from humane Eyes,
  No other fear allows,
But when the Winds that gently rise,
Doe Kiss the yielding Boughs.

Down there we satt upon the Moss,
  And did begin to play
A Thousand Amorous Tricks, to pass
  The heat of all the day.
A many Kisses he did give:
  And I return'd the same
Which made me willing to receive
  That which I dare not name.

His Charming Eyes no Aid requir'd
  To tell their softning Tale;
On her that was already fir'd,
  'Twas Easy to prevaile.
He did but Kiss and Clasp me round,
  Whilst those his thoughts Exprest:
And lay'd me gently on the Ground;
  Ah who can guess the rest?
                    APHRA BEHN
                    "The Willing Mistress"

When I was growing up, pureness was the great issue.

Instead of the world being divided up into Catholics and Protestants or Republicans and Democrats or white men and black men or even men and women, I saw the world divided into people who had slept with somebody and people who hadn't, and this seemed the only really significant difference between one person and another.

I thought a spectacular change would come over me the day I crossed the boundary line.

—SYLVIA PLATH,
The Bell Jar

When we were budding adolescents, our folklore had it that you could always recognize a nonvirgin by the whites of her eyes. We didn't know how sexual experience would be registered, exactly, but it was agreed that any red-blooded boy would know "the look" at a distance of fifty paces. We spent long and earnest hours with friends discussing who we thought was a virgin and who was not, and years went by before anyone confessed. Our predictions had been lousy. Plenty of nice girls, back then in high school, "did it," even in the era when "it" was the universal euphemism and few talked about sex out loud.

Today Sylvia Plath's concern about pureness seems quaint, a charming memory of unsophisticated days. Now people joke that virgins are an endangered species; in the Ozarks, it is said, a virgin is a five-year-old girl who can run faster than her daddy and her brothers. Once girls worried that they were misfits if they *did* have sex, and now they worry about being misfits if they *don't* have sex. Most Americans want to be in the majority, as this exchange shows:

Dear doctor: I am a teenage virgin. My boyfriend tells me that the majority of teenage girls have had sexual intercourse and I am becoming an extinct species. Am I?

Dear virgin: You represent a distinct majority (not extinct). A 1970 study by Michigan sociologists stated that, among

teenage girls, 72 percent had not had sexual intercourse. You
do what you think is right for you.
                                        —DR. NEIL SOLOMON,
                                    New York *Post,* July 6, 1976

Clearly the good doctor had generous motives behind his advice
to this insecure girl, but he should have stuck with his last sentence and left it at that. Unfortunately, he hadn't done his home-
work, or possibly his unreferenced Michigan study was based on
thirteen-year-olds; notice that neither girl nor doctor mentioned
the age of the virgins in question, and there is a gap of emotional
and experiential decades between thirteen and nineteen. The fact
is that the proportion of teenage girls who have had sexual intercourse is increasing steadily, and the age of initiation is getting
steadily younger. In one national-sample study of over 4,000 teenagers, completed in 1971 (Kantner and Zelnik), only 54 percent
of the girls were virgins by age nineteen. In a 1976 follow-up, only
45 percent were virgins by that age. And if a girl is engaged, at
whatever age, it is virtually a certainty that she will have sex with
her fiancé. All told, the ideal of virginity has been reduced to the
size of an appendix in the anatomy of national morals.

In matters of sex, attitudes and behavior don't always lie together comfortably. Betty Ford's calm remark that she would not
be surprised if her daughter had an affair created a furor far out
of proportion to her statement. The public reaction, noted writer
Anne Roiphe, "is a perfect example of how we divide what we
know into what is true and what is permissible to say out loud.
The shock waves she created were like courtesy nods in the direction of eras long past."

Indeed, if you ask people outright, they will feel obliged to
disapprove of an act that is as prevalent as dandelions. Eugene
Levitt and Albert Klassen of the Institute of Sex Research sur-
veyed a nationwide sample of 3,018 American adults in late 1970,
asking about attitudes on a range of sexual activities (see Table 2).
On the subject of premarital sex, respondents hedged their ver-
dicts, depending on the age and sex of the participants and the
degree of love between them, but the majority are basically conservative. That is, most Americans (82 percent) think that it is
always or almost always wrong for a teenage girl to have sex with

               Premarital Sex

TABLE 2.

ATTITUDES OF U.S. ADULT POPULATION TOWARD PREMARITAL INTERCOURSE
(1970 National Sample: N = 3,018)

Percentage of Americans who think premarital sex for each group is:

When premarital sex is engaged in by:	Always wrong	Almost always wrong	Wrong only sometimes/ not wrong at all
Teenage boy, in love	37%	19%	44%
Teenage boy, not in love	53	19	28
Teenage girl, in love	46	17	37
Teenage girl, not in love	68	14	18
Adult man, in love	33	14	53
Adult man, not in love	50	15	35
Adult woman, in love	36	15	49
Adult woman, not in love	55	15	30

a boy she does not love, but many fewer (47 percent) disapprove strongly of an adult man's having sex with a woman he does love. Love excuses sexual sins in some cases, they seem to be saying, but it doesn't confer a blanket pardon.

Naturally, given such attitudes and the fact that the great majority of Americans believe themselves to be "moral" and "serious" about sex, many would feel considerable conflict at the recent statistics on sexual behavior. "It appears from your report," wrote one *Redbook* reader, "that American morals are at an all-time low." Another asserted that the sexual activities of the young, the rise in premarital sex, were the cause of crime, rape, venereal disease, and Watergate.

These complaints haven't changed much over the centuries; adults have always been ready to fume about the irrepressible hedonism of the young. Consider Hesiod's mutterings, eight centuries before Christ: "I see no hope for the future of our people if they are dependent on the frivolous youth of today, for certainly all youth are reckless beyond words." Hesiod would have felt vindicated by recent American sex surveys.

Numbers are one thing, of course, and their meaning is quite another. Sexual liberals counter the conservatives' worry by arguing that the decline of the virgin does not mean the decline of civilization. On the contrary, they say, most Americans shun promiscuity and cling like barnacles to the ideal of sex with love. The ideal sexual morality has not been abandoned, it has just shifted slightly—from "good girls don't" to "good girls don't— until they are in love." Dottie, in Mary McCarthy's *The Group*, represents one tentative step toward the new philosophy:

> She and Mother had talked it over and agreed that if you were in love and engaged to a nice young man you perhaps ought to have relations once to make sure of a happy adjustment. Mother, who was very youthful and modern, knew of some very sad cases within her own circle of friends where the man and the woman just didn't fit down there and ought never to have been married. Not believing in divorce, Dottie thought it very important to arrange that side of marriage properly.

A *Redbook* reader put it this way: "In my era, ten years ago, sex with the man you intended to marry was not considered bad. But if you had more than one or two guys in a lifetime—then you were a cheap girl."

The *Redbook* survey allowed us to disentangle some facts from impressions about premarital sex in America today, to see what has changed (and what hasn't) in the behavior of young women. We were curious also to see what effect premarital sex has on a woman's married life: her overall happiness, her satisfaction with her marriage, her sexuality. Conservatives usually believe that premarital sex has a negative impact, either by unleashing immoral sexual impulses that eventually find expression in extramarital affairs, or by consuming a "nice girl" in painful repercussions of guilt and doubt. Liberals take the opposite view, arguing that premarital sex makes marriage better and stronger, by ironing out problems of adjustment beforehand, by getting oat-sowing desires out of one's system. We should not have been as surprised as we were to find that both sides were occasionally right—and both were wrong.

THE DECLINE AND FALL OF THE AMERICAN VIRGIN

> Then, why it ever happened, or how it ever happened, his arms were holding Mildred and he kissed her lips. She did not know if it was ten times or only once.
>
> She looked around—her face milk-white—to see him disappear with rapid strides through the path that had brought her there. Then she was alone.
>
> Only the birds had seen, and she could count on their discretion. She was not wildly indignant, as many would have been. Shame stunned her. But through it she gropingly wondered if she should tell the Kraummers that her chaste lips had been rifled of their innocence.
>
> —KATE CHOPIN,
> "A Shameful Affair"

In Kate Chopin's day, one hundred years ago, Mildred's kisses would have been classified as premarital sex. By the 1940s and 1950s, the battle of the sexes had moved to the back seats of cars, where the boys were aiming for more than chaste kisses. As Dan Wakefield recalls in *Going All the Way,* boys pleaded for a feel of "bare-tit" instead of the familiar "covered-tit," and girls struggled to keep the boys' hands off their breasts altogether. Most of us have memories, fond and furious, of such clumsy sessions, in which we tracked each pilgrim's progress according to the number of dates, seriousness of the suitor, and our own escalating passions. Little did we realize, however, that scientists were marking each sexual signpost as minutely as we were. We were doing so to protect our reputations, and they were doing so to advance theirs.

Thus, the study of premarital sex covers everything from kissing (French and otherwise) to "going all the way," and in between the researchers have inquired about all steps on the ladder to nirvana: petting above the waist (clothed and unclothed), petting below the waist (ditto), touching hither and thither, with and without affection. For example, James Croake and Barbara James questioned college students in 1968 and 1972 about their attitudes on thirteen sexual activities. They started off innocently asking about French Kissing, moved to Breast Fondling, Navel Fondling, Thigh Fondling, Genital Fondling, and finally to that grail of adolescent grappling, Sexual Intercourse with Orgasm. (The reader will be pleased to note that by 1972 Navel Fondling had become acceptable for "infrequent casual dating with the same person," but that most college students do not consider it appropriate on the first date.)

Actually, a good way to get a sense of how our standards have changed, and how rapidly, is to follow the topics that sex researchers have studied over the years. Premarital sex today means *sex* —intercourse—not the fondling and nuzzling that became part of the American heritage with the invention of the Model T. Few people regard the prevalence of necking as a sign of national disintegration; their worries have escalated along with their children's behavior. For that matter, some people are now saying that even the term "premarital" is dated and should be changed to "nonmarital," or just dropped. In the days when everyone married, it made sense to talk about sexual behavior before marriage. Now, with more people unattached—never married, or between marriages, or cohabiting—"premarital sex" is a concept with cobwebs.

Nevertheless, in this sample of 100,000 married women, we can safely define premarital sex as sexual intercourse before marriage. To begin with a basic fact from the survey: Eight wives out of ten said that they had had premarital sex; only two in ten were virgins at marriage. Further, we found a clear age trend, with the younger women more likely to have had sex before marriage: Sixty-eight percent of the women over age forty had done so, compared to *fully 96 percent* of the women under age twenty.

WOMEN WHO REPORTED HAVING HAD PREMARITAL INTERCOURSE

Age	Percent who had premarital sex
Under 20	96
20–24	91
25–29	84
30–34	74
35–39	74
40 and over	68

These numbers may seem astonishing, but they fit right into the results from other sex surveys over the years. The willingness of *Redbook* women to have sex with the man they plan to marry, which is virtually the universal custom among the youngest groups, is not a radical break with past traditions or a radical break with other American women. On the contrary, the *Redbook* women represent the logical evolution of a change that began at the turn of the century. Among the women Alfred Kinsey and his associates interviewed in the 1940s, almost half were virgins when they married. But 1900 was a sexual Rubicon. Women born before 1900 were far more likely to remain virgins until marriage than women born between 1900 and 1920. "Later generations," Kinsey wrote, "appear to have accepted the new pattern and maintained or expanded it."

They expanded in droves. By the 1960s most young people cheerfully endorsed the philosophy of premarital sex with love.

Sociologist Ira Reiss, in his 1960 book *Premarital Sexual Standards in America,* called the new attitude "permissiveness with affection." He added, though, that most young people were not hurrying like rabbits to translate their newly minted liberal attitudes into liberated behavior. At the height of public apprehension about the sexual revolution, Reiss calmly assured his audiences that while attitudes had changed, behavior had not. People were just talking more openly and tolerantly, he said.

Some professors thought that all the talk made inexperienced women feel that they should pretend to be knowledgeable. "I discovered that college girls were attempting to give their friends the impression that they were more sexually experienced and active than was actually the case," said James Croake. "For example, virgins would buy contraceptives and leave them on the dresser in their dormitory rooms. The typical sexual stories which men have always told were now being related by coeds who, in previous years, would have reacted in the exact opposite manner, attempting to play down or deny sexual activity."

The assumption of sexual sophistication produced new dilemmas for women, like the one Miriam faced in Marge Piercy's *Small Changes*:

> The worst moment was when he went to kiss her and she realized he would figure out she was not as experienced as she was pretending to be. She was also afraid he would think she was plain incompetent. So she decided to confess right away, before he decided she was an idiot. She was astonished then to realize he did not believe her.
>
> "Why would I make that up?"
>
> "Oh, to make it special."
>
> "But how could it not be special to me? I'm not proud of never having anything to do with men. I have to start somewhere."
>
> "Pigeon, pigeon." He put his arms around her again. "You've picked the right place to start, believe me."
>
> It was not as complicated as she would have thought, holding and touching . . . She was soon more excited than she had ever been . . . Everything seemed to go smoothly until he was lying on her and pushing against her. He tried for a

while and he stopped and explored more carefully with his finger.

"You really are a virgin."

She sat up, exasperated. "I warned you! You can't just give up now!"

Some college women may have been pretending; a good many others were not. Evidence accumulated that more was going on than researchers and parents knew. In 1966 sociologist Robert Bell was among those who believed that coeds were no more likely to be having premarital intercourse than their mothers had been. Two years later he and Jay Chaskes did a study of college women, and he changed his mind. Comparing the sexual behavior of students in 1968 with the behavior of students at the same university in 1958, Bell and Chaskes found that women had become far more ready to have sex with the man they loved.

By the 1970s, those who believed the sexual revolution was all talk and no action had to face a barrage of studies to the contrary. Consider:

• Studies of college students all over the country found that women who came of age in the 1960s were much more likely to have premarital sex than their mothers—and even than their older sisters. For example, a survey done by Shirley and Richard Jessor in 1973 found that 85 percent of the women in their sample were no longer virgins by their fourth year of college. In a two-year study of dating couples in the Boston area, psychologists Letitia Anne Peplau, Zick Rubin, and Charles Hill found that 82 percent had had intercourse.

• College women, of course, are a highly select group, not representative of all American females. But in 1971 John Kantner and Melvin Zelnik conducted a scientifically accurate survey of more than 4,000 unmarried females ages fifteen to nineteen for the Commission on Population Growth and the American Future. Theirs was a national probability sample, which means that the results can be extrapolated to cover all American women in that age group. They found that by age nineteen, 46 percent had had premarital sex—40 percent of the young white women and 80 percent of the blacks. A short five years later, 55 percent of all American girls had lost their virginity. By way of comparison,

Kinsey had found that only 18 or 19 percent of the women he interviewed had had sex by age nineteen.

• A random sample of teenagers in three Michigan communities found remarkable increases in sexual behavior in just the three years from 1970 to 1973. Arthur Vener and Cyrus Stewart questioned 4,220 students of junior-high and high-school age, and discovered that the proportion of girls who had had intercourse rose in each age group in the three-year span. For example, in 1970, 27 percent of the seventeen-year-old girls had had sex, compared to 35 percent of the girls who were seventeen in 1973. Among fifteen-year-olds, the figure jumped from 13 percent to 24 percent. Even among fourteen-year-olds, the percentage grew from 10 percent to 17 percent. These results are almost identical to those from Kantner and Zelnik's 1971 study.

Discussions of premarital sex often confuse data from people *now married* with data from people who are *still unmarried* and who therefore have not finished their "premarital" experience. Because the majority of women have premarital sex with only one man, their fiancé, studies of married women find a higher rate of premarital sex than do studies of young unmarried women. When we look at the research on wives, the *Redbook* finding that only 20 percent were virgin brides is not unusual at all. In Morton Hunt's national-sample study for the Playboy Foundation in 1972, for example, only 19 percent of the youngest wives had been virgins at marriage.

MARRIED WOMEN WHO HAD PREMARITAL SEX (Hunt, 1974)

Age	Percent
18–24	81
25–34	65
35–44	41
45–54	36
55 and over	31

THE EFFECT OF CHURCH AND SCHOOL

It appears that the question nowadays is not who does have premarital sex, but who does not. Kinsey found that in addition to a woman's age, her religious convictions went a long way toward predicting her sexual activities. "No other factors . . . affect the female's pattern of premarital behavior as markedly as the decade in which she was born and her religious background," he wrote. The effect of religion was conservative, because all of the major religions preached chastity until marriage. In Kinsey's sample, women who regularly attended church or synagogue were much less likely to have premarital sex than were women who rarely or never attended. In fact, so far as the goal of virginity went, devout Protestants, Catholics, and Jews had more in common with one another than they did with less-religious women of their own faiths. Male writers of all religious persuasions have lamented about the sexual recalcitrance of their pious girlfriends for decades; Portnoy wasn't the only adolescent with a complaint.

Across the 100,000 women in the *Redbook* survey, religious belief still has an inhibiting effect: Eighty-nine percent of the nonreligious wives had had premarital sex, compared to 61 percent of the strongly religious wives. Further, Jewish women were less likely to have had premarital sex (68.6 percent) than Catholics (78.3 percent) or Protestants (80.6 percent).

RELIGIOSITY AND PREMARITAL SEX

Religiosity	*Percent having premarital sex*
Strongly religious	61
Fairly religious	78
Mildly religious	86
Not religious	89

The remarkable thing, though, is not that religion still has an impact, but that the trend toward premarital intercourse has accelerated so rapidly even among the most devout women. Today the *most* religious women are as likely to have sex before marriage as the *least* religious women were a generation ago. For example, Kinsey found that among his nonreligious Protestants, 63 percent had had premarital sex by the age of thirty-five. That is exactly the proportion of *Redbook*'s strongly religious Protestants (ages twenty-five to thirty-five).

Table 3, for the statistically adventurous, shows how age, religious faith, and extent of religiosity intersect. Generally, the younger the woman and the weaker her religious convictions, the greater her chances of having premarital sex. Among fairly religious women under age twenty-five, for instance, 90 percent of the Protestants, 86 percent of the Catholics, and 71 percent of the Jews were not virgins at marriage. Among their nonreligious age peers, 94 percent of all three faiths had had premarital sex.

To say that religiosity and premarital sex are inversely related, however, is not the same as knowing which causes what.* It might seem most logical to assume that a religious person follows the teachings of her church and refrains as best she can from temptation. But, as many mortals can attest, sometimes, when attitude can't stop action, the action changes one's attitude. Even feelings of guilt are not enough to prevent intercourse; rather, once a girl begins to have intercourse, her feelings of guilt typically lessen. For example, Ira Reiss did a study in 1967 of a national sample of 1,500 adults and 1,000 students. He observed:

> Most young people, especially females, experience guilt at the initial stages of almost all sexual behavior. The typical experience was to feel guilty but continue the behavior and eventually come to accept it. [Nine out of ten females did not enter into sex] brashly but with serious qualms that only gradually were overcome. The guilt feelings did not seem to stop behavior, but individuals differed in the speed with which they could come to accept a particular sexual act.

*Remember that survey participants were describing their religious convictions at the time of filling out the questionnaire, not when they were growing up.

TABLE 3.

PERCENT OF REDBOOK SAMPLE WHO HAD PREMARITAL SEX, BY RELIGIOUS FAITH, DEGREE OF
RELIGIOSITY, AND AGE

Age:	Strongly religious			Fairly religious			Mildly religious			Not religious		
	-25	25–35	35+	-25	25–35	35+	-25	25–35	35+	-25	25–35	35+
Protestant	73%	63%	51%	90%	77%	67%	92%	84%	71%	94%	90%	79%
Catholic	73	57	47	86	69	58	92	81	61	94	88	70
Jewish	40	29	—[a]	71	69	36	89	71	46	94	84	56

[a]Insufficient cases.

NOTE: The proportion of agnostics and atheists who have had premarital sex is approximately the same as that of the nonreligious of all faiths.

Whether religiosity keeps a girl from having sex or whether having sex makes her less religious depends, we think, on her particular experiences and her social environment as well as the strength of her convictions. It is a rare person of any age and any sex who can withstand the influence of peers and public opinion.

One solution for women who wanted to remain virgins until marriage was simply to stop dating men who demanded sex or tried to inveigle them into it, though some paid the price of unpopularity. As one reader explained:

> My social life in college was very complicated by my personal desire to remain a virgin until marriage. That seemed totally natural to me. But most of the guys I dated felt personally insulted because I wouldn't cooperate. Men seemed to associate sex and self-approval more closely than women, who seem to know instinctively that men may desire them sexually yet not know or care about them as individuals.

To protect her virginity, she gained thirty pounds, which made her undesirable to the "sex-mad" popular boys and within reach of the shyer, less-demanding ones.

But other young women reevaluate their childhood lessons about virginity when they actually get into a love affair. Since Adam and Eve, theoretical philosophy has yielded to physical desire. And if the former is weak and the latter strong, virginity hasn't got a chance. One twenty-one-year-old wife explained why she dropped the traditional teachings of her church:

> Well, most of them just don't seem to be true. First of all, you're told that a man's sex drive is a lot stronger than a woman's—that sure is a bunch of lies. From my own experience and that of my friends, I know that it varies from individual to individual, not sex to sex. Also you are told that a boy won't "respect" you if you "go all the way" and that he'll never marry you. That too is crazy. Sure there are some guys out there who still feel hung up on that old double standard bit, but most of—no, come to think of it, *all* of my married friends had premarital intercourse with the guys they married, and most with other guys, too. And they all seem to have happy marriages!

Considering the veritable blanket of sex books, magazines, and movies that now covers the country, it is hard to remember that *Lady Chatterley's Lover* could not be published until 1960, and Henry Miller's *Tropic of Cancer* did not win its court victory until 1964. Masters and Johnson had to write up their physiological research, in *Human Sexual Response,* in impenetrable jargon so that no one could accuse them of writing pornography—and that was in 1966. Then the dam broke. Discussions, debates, and titillating descriptions began to flourish. In the lusty hothouse of the sixties, sexuality bloomed. For young people who considered religion irrelevant at best and hypocritical at worst, the question was not whether to act on the new freedom, but how soon and with whom. The wobbly ideal of premarital chastity toppled over. Literary descriptions of first intercourse began to reflect the new mood among young women, who were neither eager to lose their virginity nor able to muster new reasons to protect it. They had learned all the hands-off reflexes for self-defense, but couldn't quite remember why they should bother.

> I wouldn't let him take my dress off. I held onto it like there's some law someplace that says if you do it in a hot wool dress, it doesn't count.
>
> My hand got tired moving his hand. My mouth got tired talking. I couldn't keep up the small talk, and he couldn't keep down his desire to do what his roommate was doing.
>
> So, finally, as the sun was beginning to rise, I, Sheila Levine, let Will Fisher touch me you know where and he did you know what. Got it up there, didn't you, Will?
>
> So big deal. It hurt. No tiny spot of virgin blood on his madras spread or anything. So now I couldn't be sacrificed to the gods. . . .
>
> —GAIL PARENT,
> *Sheila Levine Is Dead and*
> *Living in New York*

Nice Jewish girls and nice Catholic girls were choosing in record numbers not to wait for a marriage license. Theologians themselves began to question the principle of premarital chastity under any circumstances, and many turned flexible—a sign of the times.

In 1964 theologian Harvey Cox, writing in the magazine *Christianity and Crisis,* rejected the idea that premarital sex could be reduced to a simple yes-or-no decision. "By definition 'premarital' refers to people who plan to marry someone some day. Pre-marital sexual conduct should therefore serve to strengthen the chances of sexual success and fidelity in marriage. And we must face the real question of whether avoidance of intercourse beforehand is always the best preparation." Without waiting for a response from the nation's pulpits, the majority of religious women in the sixties had decided that the real answer was no.

Kinsey found that the more education a woman had, the more likely she was to have had premarital sex. Thus, 70 percent of his interviewees who had a grade-school education were virgins at marriage, compared to 53 percent of the high-school graduates and only 40 percent of those who finished college. But then Kinsey took the next step, and found out why the less educated had the least premarital experience: They married earlier than girls who stayed in school. When Kinsey compared groups of women on the basis of their age at marriage (sixteen to twenty, twenty-one to twenty-five, and twenty-six to thirty), he discovered that the same proportions in each category had had premarital sex, regardless of how much schooling they had had. It was age of marriage, not level of education, that told the story. But Kinsey could not determine which caused what: Did intercourse lead to marriage, or did the imminence of marriage lead to intercourse? Did early sex and marriage cause a girl to drop out of school, or did leaving school prompt a girl to have early affairs in search of a safe marriage?

In the *Redbook* study, education made no difference in the chances of a woman's having premarital sex; roughly four out of five women at all levels of education had done so. But education did have an impact, all right; not on whether a woman would have sex before marriage, but on when.

NOT WHETHER, BUT WHEN: AGE AT INITIATION

The big change among young women today is that they are no longer restricting their sexual experiences to the year or so before marriage, as Kinsey had found. In increasing numbers, they have their sexual initiation three to five years before they marry.

AGE AT FIRST INTERCOURSE

Age of initiation	Percent
Under 16	13
16–17	36
18–19	33
20–21	12
22 and over	6

Early research did not attach much importance to a girl's age at first sexual intercourse. Virginity was the question, and, like pregnancy, virginity had a yes-or-no answer. In Kinsey's volume on female sexuality, the researchers did not think to ask whether age at initiation was related to later sexual behavior—before marriage, in marriage, or outside of marriage. One reason was that not enough early-teenage girls were having sex; among women born before the turn of the century, only 2 percent had had premarital sex by age fifteen. This proportion did not change among women born between 1900 and 1920, but Kinsey noted, without comment, that the number doubled to 4 percent of the women born in the 1920s. Today that 4 percent has more than trebled. According to the nationwide Kantner and Zelnik study conducted in 1971, 14 percent of all American girls have had intercourse by age fifteen (very close to *Redbook*'s 13 percent). And Zelnik and Kantner's 1976 study indicates that this figure is still rising—in 1976, 18 percent of all American girls had had intercourse by age fifteen.

We were surprised to find that strength of religious belief had no effect on a girl's age of first intercourse. That means that the strongly religious woman and the nonreligious woman were equally likely to have waited until age twenty to have premarital sex, or to have started at age fifteen. One third of the most religious women, for example, were sexually experienced by age sixteen or

TABLE 4.
PROPORTION OF WIVES HAVING PREMARITAL SEX, BY
LEVEL OF EDUCATION AND AGE OF SEXUAL INITIATION

| Age of first intercourse | *Highest level of education completed* | | | |
	Grade school	High school graduate	Some college	College degree or advanced degree
15 and under	59%	20%	9%	7%
16–17	28	49	32	19
18–19	10	23	43	31
20–21	1	5	12	27
22 and over	2	3	5	16

seventeen. So were one third of the fairly religious women, the mildly religious, and the nonreligious. Although we noted that very religious women were the most likely to be virgins at marriage, apparently once they decided to have sex the timing was not an issue.

Although religiosity did not influence age of initiation, education did, with far greater impact than Kinsey had found. The longer a woman stays in school, the longer she typically waits to have premarital sex (and vice versa). Of the *Redbook* wives who have postgraduate degrees, more than one fourth remained virgins until they were at least twenty-two years old; but only 2 percent of the wives with grade-school educations waited that long. Conversely, the girls who were most apt to have sex by age fifteen also tended to stop going to school. As Table 4 shows, fully 59 percent of the wives with only a grade-school education had had sex by age fifteen, compared with 20 percent of the high-school-graduate group and only 7 percent of the college graduates.*

Why? Maybe girls who have high academic ambitions find

---

*The impact of education in delaying sexual experience explains why Jewish girls are somewhat more likely to be older (average 18.3 years) at first intercourse than Catholics (average 17.9 years) and Protestants (17.6 years). It is not that Jewish girls are more religious; they are not. But they are more apt to go on to college and graduate school (42 percent) than either Catholics (20 percent) or Protestants (25 percent).

themselves on the fringes of the popularity parade, passed over by boys who don't want the brainy type. Maybe their educational motives and their sexual ones don't mesh until college. Maybe their school and family environments place more emphasis on education and less emphasis on sex. Perhaps girls who have neither the money nor the motivation for college place their hopes in sexual relationships and an early marriage.

Whatever the chain of events, we can deduce from the *Redbook* data that some important consequences follow from the age at first intercourse—*and fifteen is the magic number.* As we said earlier, girls who have sex at that age or younger are significantly different from their sisters who wait even one year longer.

The Precocious Fifteens

Theoretically, the younger a girl is when she first has sex, the more years she has to experiment sexually before marriage. So we would expect girls who started earlier to have more lovers before they married (Table 5). But it doesn't turn out quite that simply.

TABLE 5.
NUMBER OF PREMARITAL LOVERS, BY AGE AT FIRST
INTERCOURSE

Number of partners	*Age at first intercourse*				
	–15	*16–17*	*18–19*	*20–21*	*21+*
1	30%	47%	57%	66%	62%
2–5	39	37	32	25	29
6–10	17	10	6	4	9
More than 10	15	7	5	4	0

In fact, the women who had sex by age fifteen are the most sexually active. Twice as many of them had more than ten lovers, for example, as did their peers who had waited just one more year for their first premarital sex (15 percent to 7 percent). Thirty-two percent of the precocious fifteen-year-olds had more than six lovers before marriage, but only 8 percent of the women who were virgins until age twenty or later had that many lovers.

The assumption that earlier sex leads to more partners does not really hold up, once we discount the youngest group. That is, if we know that one woman had her first sexual experience at age sixteen or seventeen, while another was twenty-one, we would have a fifty-fifty chance of predicting which one had the greater number of lovers. The fifteens represent a significant break with the other women.

Some people would regard the apparent "promiscuity" of the girls who have sex by age fifteen as further evidence of the sexual revolution (if they're liberal) or of the nation's moral decay (if they're conservative). Neither view is correct. We found no *generational* trend toward more premarital lovers: Age fifteen is the critical age, regardless of whether a woman now is twenty or forty. In other words, wives now in their forties who first had sex at age fifteen had the same number of partners as younger wives who also had an early sexual initiation.

Further, the proportion of women who have only one lover before marriage, their fiancé, has remained remarkably constant over the generations. In Kinsey's study, slightly more than half of the married women had had one premarital partner. This figure was the same in Hunt's 1972 national study. And the same in the *Redbook* study, across age groups.

The Promiscuity Question

As sex researchers like to say, most people call "promiscuous" anyone who has had one more lover than they did. (It's the same with "excessive" sex, as in the example of the Victorian lady who thought masturbation was acceptable if not done to excess—more than once a month. She herself masturbated once a month.) By whatever definition, promiscuity is not increasing markedly among young people. Among most American women today, sex is still carefully connected to love and marriage, not with the thrills of sexual adventure for its own sake. Only 8 percent of the respondents, for example, had one-night stands with several lovers before they were married.

And yet the experience of the women who had sex by age fifteen

NUMBER OF LOVERS FOR WOMEN HAVING PREMARITAL SEX

Number of Lovers	Kinsey (1953)	Total Redbook (1974)	Redbook *by age*			
			20–24	25–34	35–39	40+
1	53%	51%	53%	50%	56%	51%
2–5	34	34	33	33	31	36
6–10	7	9	9	9	7	7
More than 10	6	6	6	7	7	5

may be a harbinger of life styles to come. Although they are still a small minority, their numbers are growing. They are important because their lives seem to be characterized by a high level of sexual energy and experimentation—and personal unhappiness. We divided the respondents who had had premarital sex into groups, according to their age at initiation: fifteen and under, sixteen or seventeen, eighteen to twenty-one, and over twenty-one. Then we compared the answers of each group on many survey questions about sexual experience and satisfaction.

We found that the women who had had sex at the youngest ages were more sexually charged, both in their premarital lives and after marriage. Once married, they were the most likely to use devices for sexual stimulation (vibrators, oils, feathers), to have sex while high on marijuana, to masturbate frequently, to try new sexual positions and variations, and to be turned on by pornography. These women were also more likely to have had a homosexual encounter at least once (8 percent, compared to 3 percent of the total sample), and to have enjoyed it.

Unfortunately, all of this sexual activity is not making them happier, either with their sex lives or with their marriages. As one wife wrote, "I was 15 when I first had intercourse, but I was so dumb I did not know what was expected of me. As far as I'm concerned, the first three lovers do not even count. I certainly did not enjoy it. I was married at 17 and even though I had had relations with several men I was still dumb." She finally worked out a happy adjustment with her husband, but in that she was fortunate. The women who had their sexual initiation at age fifteen or younger were the *least* likely to rate their marriages and marital sex as good. And although they have intercourse just as often as other wives, they are more likely to think they aren't getting sex often enough. Finally, more of these women describe themselves as "mostly unhappy" than their peers do. More of them got divorced and remarried.

One of the frustrating things about large-scale surveys like this one is that what they give with one hand they take away with the other. In this case, the data create an unexpected statistical portrait of sexually active fifteen-year-olds who are different sexually from girls who do not have intercourse until they are sixteen or older. But the survey does not say why they are different. Maybe girls who have sex in their early teens reach physical maturity earlier, but their emotional maturity does not keep pace. Maybe they come from troubled families and throughout their lives use sex to find security and comfort. One wife explained:

> My premarital experience was very limited in quality, though I did have intercourse once each with three different men and two rather long-term affairs. One affair was more a friendship, where sex was a way of sharing warmth and making my friend satisfied, but to me the relationship was not satisfying sexually. The other affair was not satisfying either, but a year spent filling an emotional hunger for ultimate closeness and touching—physical unity.

She, like over one third of the other sexually precocious wives, did not reach orgasm during her premarital experience.

Now that is a possibly ominous finding. If more sex does not mean better sex, young women are simply replacing one set of inhibiting rules with another. Queen Victoria casts a long shadow. The important thing is to be able to answer the questions posed by these readers: "Are premarital experiences pleasant, ecstatic, loving, fulfilling or a big disappointment, disgusting, forced? Do young girls have intercourse because they are sexually aroused— or because they feel it is the thing to do, that it will ensure future dates?" "Now if I went back to those days [before my marriage], knowing what I know now about sex and love, I think I would have had more experiences—physical as well as love relationships.

But I wonder if I could handle a free sexual atmosphere. I mean, are the girls today really free from that ridiculous guilt imposed on us, or do they just *say* they are?"

PLEASURE, PASSION, AND THE BIG O

Guilt is a muzzy feeling to get hold of under the best of circumstances, and positively elusive in relation to sex. For one thing, it is often hard to distinguish women who really do feel guilty about premarital sex from those who think they should feel guilty but don't. And it is hard to distinguish women who feel so guilty that their pleasure and sexual responses are totally inhibited from women whose guilt does not interfere with their satisfaction—or who regard guilt as a vestigial emotion from childhood training and intend to shed it as rapidly as their clothes. As Reiss found, most women have some tremors of guilt in their early sexual experience, but guilt has little to do with their decisions about intercourse.

The women whose guilt is sustained in spite of their experience tend to have come from sexually repressive homes. One conflicted wife wrote:

> Although I had premarital sex, I have always regretted it. When I was a child, sex was a dirty word in our house, strictly verboten. I have tried to create a different atmosphere about it with my own children, a son age 24 and two girls age 14 and 17. I answered that I don't want my son or daughters to have premarital sex, but I know that my son has been having sex for at least six years. It puts one in a strange predicament.

This woman has apparently not been able to conquer her ambivalence about sex even yet.

However, for every woman who feels guilty because she had sex before marriage, there is at least one who regrets that she didn't. One wife who had an unhappy first marriage wrote, "If I had it to do over again I would have intercourse with several men before I married, and so I do not condemn girls today for doing so."

Another woman, who said that she had grown up feeling guilty about sex and wasn't "liberated" until her late thirties, added that she certainly hoped her children would feel free to have premarital sex without "fear, guilt, harm, and fuss."

One measure of a woman's comfort about premarital sex is her wishes for her children. The respondents were not unequivocally in favor, but neither were they completely opposed. Overall, they still held to the double standard, with nearly twice as many women being opposed to their daughter's having premarital sex as those to their son's (25 percent to 14 percent). Almost four in ten women, though, were uncertain about whether they would object to or support their children's decision on this matter. This is in spite of the fact that eight in ten of them had had premarital sex themselves.

	Would you object to a son's having premarital sex?	*Would you object to a daughter's premarital sex?*
Yes	14%	25%
No	47	33
Don't know	39	42

A more direct indication of the quality of their premarital sex lives is, naturally, the likelihood of reaching orgasm. In this country the National Orgasm Barometer is read every few months or so as a measure of health and happiness, and while it may seem that people have gone quite berserk about climaxes, there is a reason behind their madness. Female sexuality has been so taboo, and women's responsiveness so repressed, that it has literally taken years for adult women to undo the inhibitions of their youth. Kinsey observed that the girl who spends her adolescence "withdrawing from physical contacts and tensing her muscles in order to avoid response" becomes conditioned, and does not shed the association of arousal/tension easily, even after marriage. In his sample, one fourth of the women never reached orgasm during coitus in their first year of marriage, and only 39 percent almost always did. But practice makes perfect, though sometimes practice takes a long time. By the fifteenth year of marriage, 45 percent of the women in Kinsey's sample almost always reached orgasm, and only 12 percent were completely nonorgasmic.

The fact is that female sexual response is much more susceptible to learning and cultural overlays than male sexuality, for anatomical reasons as well as social ones. No books need to teach males how to masturbate; their pleasure principle is right out there in public view. No books need to teach males what an erection is; they cleverly can deduce when they are aroused. And no books need to tell a man what an orgasm is; his orgasm often has a mind of its own, and will come when it will come. But many women have a lot to learn:

> "You *came*, Boston," he remarked, with the air of a satisfied instructor. Dottie glanced uncertainly at him; could he mean that thing she had done that she did not like to think about? "I beg your pardon," she murmured. "I mean you had an orgasm." Dottie made a vague, still-inquiring noise in her throat; she was pretty sure, now, she understood, but the new word discombobulated her. "A climax," he added, more sharply. "Do they teach you that word at Vassar?" "Oh," said Dottie, almost disappointed that that was all there was to it. "Was that . . . ?" She could not finish the question. "That was it," he nodded. "That is, if I am a judge." "It's normal then?" she wanted to know, beginning to feel better. . . .
>
> —MARY MCCARTHY,
> *The Group*

The *Redbook* survey found signs that the learning is easier for young women today. It still takes them a while to become regularly orgasmic, but fewer say that they never reached orgasm in their premarital affair(s).* Inhibitions seem to be lifting over the

---

*The survey question asked, "In your premarital sexual experience, how often did you reach orgasm?" Answers should be taken with a grain of subjective salt, because the women were calling up memories from years past. Their answers may be influenced by current marital happiness or dissatisfaction, feelings of guilt or passionate love that accompanied the experience, and so on.

generations: a large proportion of women over age thirty-five (41 percent) said they never had orgasms during premarital sex, compared to 29 percent of the women under age twenty-five. On the other hand, the number of young women who always reach orgasm is still low. One new bride said, "I never reached orgasm before my marriage because I was really against premarital sex at the time, and I only enjoyed sex after my first experience with my husband."

TABLE 6.

AMONG WOMEN HAVING PREMARITAL SEX, PERCENT WHO
REACHED ORGASM, BY AGE OF RESPONDENT

	Age of respondent		
Percent who reached orgasm	*–24*	*25–34*	*35+*
Always	7%	6%	9%
Most of the time	27	21	19
Sometimes	38	38	31
Never	29	35	41

Kinsey found that religion acted as a sexual suppressant, not just in the likelihood of a woman's having intercourse, but in the likelihood of her enjoying it. In his sample, devoutly religious women of all faiths tended to feel guilty about sex, express regrets if they had sex before marriage, and be less orgasmic than nonreligious women. We tested his finding, and discovered that it no longer holds. Among *Redbook* readers, religious women were as orgasmic as the nonreligious; for example, devout Catholics were as likely to reach orgasm during intercourse as lapsed Catholics, even in premarital experiences. Religious belief may cause a woman to delay her first intercourse, but once she begins her love affair she is as likely to reach orgasm as her agnostic friends.

Plus ça change . . . Nevertheless, some things about female sexual response haven't changed. For most women, orgasm depends on being in love and feeling comfortable with their lovers.

The *Redbook* women who had had premarital sex on a casual basis—once or a few times with several partners—were apparently not doing so for pure sexual pleasure, as they were the *least* likely to be reaching orgasm. The women who were *most* likely to be orgasmic in their premarital experience were having sex in a regular, stable relationship. Among the women who had had a series of one-night stands, for example, fully 77 percent said they never reached orgasm, compared to 23 percent of the women who had sex frequently with their partners. What matters in premarital responsiveness is not the number of lovers, actually, but the number of times with each one. As it ever was in this society, the great majority of young women need a sustained sense of intimacy, security, and trust from a relationship before they shake off inhibitions and respond sexually. They seem to need the illusion, if not the reality, of imminent marriage. Doris Lessing, for one, had an opinion about this facet of female psychology:

> And what about us? Free, we say, yet the truth is they get erections when they're with a woman they don't give a damn about, but we don't have an orgasm unless we love him. What's free about that?
>
> 　　　　　　　　　　　　　　—DORIS LESSING,
> 　　　　　　　　　　　　　　*The Golden Notebook*

PREMARITAL NOW, ADULTERY LATER?

A religious mother of three wrote: "Monogamy and fidelity are for me the way to happiness. If a couple has love, trust, and mutual respect for each other, experimenting beforehand is not necessary. Their sex lives will work out naturally."

A puzzled sixteen-year-old wrote: "I would like to know if premarital sex has anything to do with your later marriage? I have heard a lot about men wanting the women they marry to be virgins but I have found out that they don't really care as long as they were the first ones their wives-to-be ever had intercourse with."

Premarital sex neither improves the chances of marital success nor destroys them. Since so many young women today do have sex before marriage, it may be moot even to discuss the question of the effects of premarital sex. But so long as conservatives and liberals drag out this warhorse for their particular battles, it is worth a look at the data.

A generation ago Kinsey gave ammunition to those who argued that "immoral" behavior before marriage caused further "immorality" after marriage: The women he interviewed who had had premarital sex were somewhat more likely to have had extramarital sex than were women who were virgins at marriage. Specifically, 29 percent of those who had sex before marriage also had had an extramarital affair, compared to only 13 percent of those who had not had premarital sex. (However, the women were not promiscuous either after marriage or before, limiting themselves to one or two partners in either case.)

In the *Redbook* sample, women who had had an extramarital affair were somewhat more likely to have had sex before marriage, but this result hardly warrants a shout from the rooftops. By way of contrast: Thirty wives in every 100 who replied had had an extramarital affair, and of those 30, 26 had had premarital sex also. On the other hand, of the 70 wives in 100 who had *not* had extramarital sex, 55 had had premarital sex. Premarital sex may increase the odds of extramarital sex, but far fewer women indulge in the latter than enjoy the former. Further, it turned out that it was not premarital sex per se that was related to extramarital affairs, but the age at which premarital sex first occurred. Again it was those experimental fifteen-year-olds who were far and away more likely to have had extramarital affairs, and more extramarital lovers, than the women who had their first sexual experience in their late teens.

Well, then, does premarital sex make for a happier marriage or a better married sex life? Does experience beforehand get the problems ironed out or create new problems? The answer, in this survey, is that *premarital sex has absolutely no effect on a woman's marriage.* That means that for every woman who feels benefited by having sex before marriage, another does not. It means that of all the many factors that go into a good marriage and a good sex life, premarital sex is not one of them. It means that some women have perfectly happy marriages although they were virgins on their wedding day, and that others are perfectly happy to have experimented to their hearts' and bodies' content. The objective fact of premarital sex has little connection to one's marriage; it is the subjective emotions that count. If a woman truly believes that she should wait until her wedding day, or if she knows that she wants much experience before settling down, she creates a self-fulfilling prophecy. What she expects is what she gets.

THE PILL AND THE MODERN TEENAGER

I am only 15 years old and considered by many people to be too young to read such things or to even know about such things. I masturbate quite often. I am not a virgin. I have only had sexual intercourse two times; I enjoyed it although there was never any emotional tie. What I did those two times was not making love, it was sexual—purely sexual. It was a great relief to me to know that the things I do are not so odd as I thought.

I wish my 14-year-old daughter would not read [your article]. It seems to say, especially to an impressionable teenager, that if you don't have sex outside marriage you are a freak, a chicken, or hopelessly old-fashioned.

Parents and children often have as much trouble communicating about sex as lovers do. Some adults take the view that if they don't talk about it, their children won't discover it. The ostrich strategy allows some parents to rationalize that their children are too young or not ready to learn about sex, and others to decide that their children know more than is good for them. The teenagers, meanwhile, blunder along, trying to chart a sexual course in hormonally stormy seas.

At the age of 16 I had my first encounter with the complete sexual act, only because I had not been informed by my parents or other adults as to what it was. My sexual education up to that point included everything except the human aspect of it. From then on I got my sexual education from first-hand experience.

One adult misconception about the young is that a major factor in the teenage sexual revolution was the birth-control pill. But social scientists have demonstrated that the decision to have sex has little to do with knowledge or availability of birth control. Kristin Moore and Steven Caldwell recently prepared a report for the Urban Institute, carefully analyzing the data from Kantner and Zelnik's 1971 study. They wanted to see whether the national decline in the age of first intercourse among teenage girls was related to access to birth control, abortion, and welfare benefits. None of these factors influenced a girl's chances of having premarital sex. As Ira Reiss found in his 1970 research, many young women would rather be sorry than safe, if safe requires unromantic premeditation. "Many females use the rhythm method," he wrote, "fully aware that it is one of the less effective methods and that better methods are available, but this is the method that conforms to their values."

Remember the name for people who use the rhythm method? Parents. Especially for people who don't know how the rhythm method is synchronized with the menstrual cycle. Kantner and Zelnik found that the majority of all American teenage girls did not know that mid-cycle is the time of greatest risk of conception. About half of them held a dangerous belief, that the highest risk occurs just before or after menstruation. As young white teenagers acquired more experience and education, their knowledge of the menstrual cycle improved, but only 56 percent of the college-educated whites knew the right answer.

In a 1977 update of their 1971 study, Kantner and Zelnik report that the proportion of teenagers having premarital sex had climbed another 30 percent by 1976, but that their understanding of the biological facts of life had not improved. Few of these young women used contraception when they first began to have intercourse, and a significant percentage didn't use any form of contraception until after they had their first unwanted pregnancy. But it's a good sign that more teenagers are using better birth control once they become sexually active, and as a result of contraception and abortion the escalating illegitimacy rate is beginning to decline. While only 45 percent of all sexually active teenage girls had used contraception (in their most recent act of intercourse) in 1971, 63 percent had done so by 1976. Further, use of more reliable methods, namely the pill and the IUD, increased from 16 percent to 33 percent.

It is clear that nothing short of government-issued chastity belts will halt the trend toward earlier premarital sexual experience. Moore and Caldwell asked their computer to predict the proportion of twenty-year-old virgins in 1982, and the computer, chewing on its national statistics, answered, "Two percent." We should add that its prediction for the number of virgins in 1976 was precisely on target.

Given these facts of life, it is important to understand the experience of the girls who begin sexual intercourse in their early teens, because their sexual precocity does not always bring them pleasure. Instead, they tend to fall into early marriages and early pregnancies (often in reverse order), have babies, have lovers, and have divorces. They are not especially happy. Surely this is not the goal of sexual liberation. But one wife's history suggests what premarital sex can and does accomplish for many women:

> Until I established my own sexual identity and learned that I had sexual rights, my enjoyment was much less great than it is now. My past experiences have done much to establish my present sexual attitudes and they have done much for my marriage. Sex is an added enjoyment for us, not our sole occupation with each other. Premarital sex gave me self-confidence, and taught me about my body. By the time we married I was worrying less and enjoying it more.

A SUMMARY OF THE PREMARITAL SCENE: OLD NEWS AND
NEW NEWS

Old News	*New News*
1. Most women still have premarital sex only with their fiancés . . .	1. . . . but more and more women are having premarital sex, which is expected soon to be a virtually universal experience.
2. Most teenage girls do not have sex on a casual or promiscuous basis . . .	2. . . . but teenage girls are having their first sexual intercourse at younger ages.
3. Most girls still need time, love, and learning before they become regularly orgasmic . . .	3. . . . but fewer girls are nonorgasmic in their premarital sex experiences than women were in previous generations.
4. Many women still cling to the double standard for their children . . .	4. . . . but premarital sex with love has become the accepted behavior for both sexes.
5. Girls who begin intercourse at fifteen or younger are more likely to have numerous lovers (before and after marriage), to be sexually adventuresome, and to be less happy with their marriages and sex lives . . .	5. . . . but this has always been true of girls who have an early sexual initiation; it is not necessarily the wave of the future.
6. Premarital sex does not affect a woman's satisfaction with her marriage or her married sex life.	6. Premarital sex does not affect a woman's satisfaction with her marriage or her married sex life.

3
MARITAL SEX

Will he never come calling falling climbing careless dareful
rising spreading me wide
when will he rage foaming roaming the tunneling stair
to fling me high up beside him where
the saddle shines damp with darkbright desire
by rosebrush aflame with thorny desire
on softest fire   on sharpest fire
love's steed bestride   together to ride
Ah gallop oh gallop hoh gallop us clear!
slow, whoa . . . hohum again here
so home to the stable the sugar the sniff
down to the plain from the sheermounting cliff
                    —EVE MERRIAM,
                        The Lovemaking: His and Hers

There is in our house but one bed, too large for you, a bit narrow for the two of us. It is chaste, white, bare; no draperies, in the light of day, veil its honest candor. Those who come to visit us regard it tranquilly, with no furtive, conspiratorial side glances, because it slopes in the middle to a single soft valley, like the bed of a young girl who sleeps alone. They little know, those who enter here, that every night our two bodies press deeper, under its luxurious shroud . . .

Now I lie quiet, my head against your shoulder.

How my heart beats! And yours too, I can hear it thudding away under my cheek. Aren't you asleep? I raise my head a little, I dimly make out the paleness of your head thrown back, the tawny shadow of your hair. Your knees are as cool as two oranges . . .

I know, oh, how well, that you will tighten your embrace, and that, if the cradling of your arms does not suffice to calm me, your kiss will hold me faster still, your hands grow more soothing, and your love will be a sovereign spell that will drive from me all the demons of fever, anger, and unrest. . . .

—COLETTE,
"Nuit Blanche"

It's hard to find a good love story about a married couple. Aside from the Duke and Duchess of Windsor, the love stories that grip the public imagination are about passionate adolescents (Romeo and Juliet), unconsummated adorations (Don Quixote and Dulcinea), or hopeless triangles (Sir Lancelot, Guinevere, and King Arthur). Once sex and passion go legitimate, one is to infer, they fade like yesterday's news. Even Friar Lawrence consoles Juliet's grieving parents with the reminder: "She's not well married that lives married long;/ But she's best married that dies married young."

Marriage, in short, has had a bad press. Poets, philosophers, and husbands have whined so much about it that it is remarkable that so many people manage to get dragged to the altar. Shelley: "A system could not well have been devised more studiously hostile to human happiness than marriage." Benjamin Disraeli: "Every woman should marry—and no man." Henry Mayhew: "Advice to persons about to marry—don't." Oscar Wilde: "Men marry because they are tired, women because they are curious; both are disappointed." "Who marries does well," says an anonymous proverb, "who marries not does better."

Now social scientists have added to the arsenal of ammunition against marriage. Sociologist Jessie Bernard and many others marshal evidence to show how marriage whittles housewives into mere shadows of their former selves. Marriage, the studies show, erodes the self-esteem and self-confidence of women as it enhances those of men: Married men are better off, physically and psychologically, than single men, while married women are worse off than their single peers. Married men earn more and advance further in their careers than single men do; the reverse is true for women.

In spite of this evidence, both sexes believe that marriage is the key to happiness. Psychologist Angus Campbell at the University of Michigan found that even though single women are healthier than housewives, they are not especially happier. Apparently many people in this society feel that marriage will solve their problems and bring happiness; no matter how good (or bad) their lives, marriage makes things better.

Thomas Jefferson included an artful dodge in the Declaration of Independence when he asserted human rights to "life, liberty, and the pursuit of happiness." He did not promise us happiness, you notice; he merely said we ought to feel free to chase after it. He probably should have stayed with his original formulation on behalf of life, liberty, and *property,* the last being somewhat more tangible than happiness. As it was, he set the nation on an impossible quest. Americans pursue happiness the way they play tennis: earnestly, feverishly, and virtually as a full-time avocation. Happiness has become the national ambition, right up there with wealth. The irony, naturally, is that you can't nab happiness directly; it will always elude a frontal attack. You have to sneak up on it sideways, as if you were looking for something else.

Studies find that the main ingredients of happiness are money, love, and sex (not necessarily in that order). But there is also a strong psychological component. Happiness is as much a matter of what you *think* you have as of what you *actually* have. Like sexual security, it rests on comparisons with others and on expectations. But these days expectations face in different directions, like Dr. Doolittle's pushme-pullyu. A good sex life and a good marriage are both supposed to bring bliss, but everyone knows that you can't have a good sex life if you're married—right? Proverbs all over the world have enshrined that tiny bit of folk wisdom. "Marriage is fever in reverse; it starts with heat and ends with cold," says the German version; "a dish o' married love soon grows cauld," runs the Scottish equivalent.

The *Redbook* readers have a few good things to say about sex in marriage to counter these surly sayings. Among them:

• The length of marriage does not diminish love or lessen a wife's happiness. Newlyweds, of course, are the most euphoric people in the world, but after the first year of marriage the percentage of happy or unhappy wives does not change significantly, no matter how long they have been married. Women married more than ten years are as happy with themselves, their marriages, and their sex lives as women married only a year or two. Indeed, some of the most sexually satisfied wives are in their sixties and seventies. Married love has not grown cold for this group, even though the heat of the honeymoon subsides.

TABLE 7.
SATISFACTION WITH SEX LIFE BY NUMBER OF YEARS MARRIED

	Years of marriage			
Marital sex is	*Less than 1*	*1–4*	*5–10*	*More than 10*
Very good/good	80%	68%	66%	65%
Fair	17	23	21	20
Poor/very poor	3	9	13	15

• Age has nothing to do with overall happiness. The oldest wives are as happy as the youngest.

• A good sex life is essential to a happy marriage. A few women say that they have fine marriages but lousy sex lives, but their stoicism suits only a small minority. Victorian expectations—you had a good marriage if your husband didn't beat you and provided for the family—have gone the way of the antimacassar. Among the *Redbook* readers, *none* of the women who rated their marriages as very good said their sex lives were very bad, and, conversely, none of the women whose marriages were very bad said their sex lives were very good. If you've got one, you've just about got the other.

• The incidence of homosexual experience has apparently not

changed much in the last generation, in spite of the considerable discussion and the new militancy of gay people. Kinsey found that only 3 percent of all married women had had a homosexual encounter by age forty-five, although the rate was somewhat higher for single, widowed, and divorced women. In the *Redbook* survey, similarly, 3 percent had had a homosexual experience in adulthood: 1.7 percent had done so only once, 0.8 percent had done so occasionally, and only 0.4 percent had homosexual relations often.

• Women who work outside the home are as happy with their marriages and their sex lives as housewives are. An outside job did not affect the frequency of intercourse or sexual satisfaction.

There is a built-in problem to research on happiness, however. Social scientists know that if you ask people whether they are happy, you can just about guarantee that some 75 to 80 percent of them will say yes. Less than 10 percent will say their lives are miserable or their marriages disastrous. These percentages hold for samples of the entire American population (such as Angus Campbell's) as well as in smaller studies. In the *Redbook* sample, only 6 percent of the wives said their marriages were poor, only 9 percent said they were personally unhappy most of the time, and only 12 percent said their sex lives were bad. Are these figures accurate? Optimistic souls say: How marvelous that most of our population feel so good! What a jolly nation we are! Cynical researchers doubt the numbers. They point out that almost everyone wants to present a happy countenance, even to oneself, and that to admit dissatisfaction and unhappiness means having to confront the reasons. They observe that although housewives and employed wives say they are equally happy, many surveys find that housewives have a much higher rate of psychosomatic symptoms: nervous tension, insomnia, stomachache, dizziness, headache, depression and anxiety, and so on. Many of these women are like William Hazlitt, a nineteenth-century writer whose assessment of his experiences was quite out of synch with the reality. As Morton Hunt recalls, Hazlitt's years "were filled with domestic discord, unrequited love, money troubles and ill health, but [he] said in all earnestness, as he lay expiring, 'Well, I have had a happy life!' "

Because of the difficulty of interpreting overall self-reports of satisfaction—and one women's joy is another's misery—many sex researchers turn to the objective, measurable aspects of sexual experience. They prefer to count orgasms or sexual episodes as indicators of happiness. Others say that sexual satisfaction is all in the mind, not the genitals. What makes for good sex? Experimentation, variety, frequency? Is more better? Is less more?

A DIGRESSION: TWO WOMEN

> I answered this to have it known that there are normal human beings still living normal lives in our nation. Sex is a normal, healthy thing that enriches life and unites husband and wife and builds a happy, satisfying family. Most of these questions are sick, sick, and if such things exist the nation is well on its way to collapse.

The "sick, sick" practices of sex, to this woman, are oral sex, anal sex, masturbation, pornography, wearing erotic clothes for one's husband, using vibrators or oils for sexual stimulation, having sex during the day or anywhere other than the bedroom, having sex before marriage, and . . . well, her list probably surpasses the number of questions that could fit into the survey.

Yet this woman describes her sex life and her marriage as very good. She was a virgin at marriage and has had no lover other than her husband. They have sex once a week, a frequency she thinks is just right. She says that foreplay is not necessary for her to become aroused, that she always reaches orgasm during intercourse, that she plays an active part sexually, and that she and her husband often discuss their sexual feelings and desires. She is over forty, has been married for fifteen years, has an advanced degree, and earns over twenty-five thousand dollars a year. She is, she says, very happy. There is nothing she dislikes about her sex life.

In contrast, consider this letter from a Southern wife, also employed, also married for fifteen years:

> The preoccupation with sex has made me sick. Anyone who would make a study of human sex practices the way [Masters and Johnson] have must be sick. There is a Bible you know,

and it gives us information on every segment of our lives. Women in this country, while loudly proclaiming their place in the world, have lowered their position to animal-like existence.

For all her remarks about survey-takers, she sent along her questionnaire, and no wonder that she is sick of sex; she gave her marriage and her sex life the lowest rating. Although her sexual behavior is not much different from that of the first woman—they both list the same taboos, for example—she thinks her husband wants sex too often, possibly because she reaches orgasm only once in a while.

These two women are both rigid about "proper" sexual behavior. Both believe sex should not be discussed publicly, but both filled out the questionnaire. Both have had sex with only one man. One feels sexually satisfied, the other does not. For one, the belief that certain sexual practices are sick does not affect her own enjoyment; for the other, the same belief masks frustration and blocks her ability to change. She rationalizes her unhappiness by saying that women who want sexual pleasure lead an "animal-like" life. (If one has to suffer sexual deprivation, better to make a moral virtue of it.) Both women talk about sexual sickness, but only one has it.

Clearly, there is more to good sex than meets the body.

INGREDIENTS OF GOOD SEX, PART I: WHAT HAPPENS IN BED

QUALITY VERSUS QUANTITY

The whole country has had its sexual batteries recharged in the last decade. According to Princeton University's Office of Population Research, which worries about such things, sex is on the rise. Interviews with a national sample of married women found that between 1965 and 1970 there was a 14 percent increase in frequency of lovemaking, and the new numbers are expected to show another jump.

The statistics alone wouldn't be all that interesting, but it turns out that more sex does mean better sex. In the *Redbook* sample, the higher the frequency of intercourse, the happier the wives were with their marriages and the better they rated their sex lives. Cause and effect become circular in this case, naturally, like a serpent swallowing its tail: The more you like it, the more often you do it, and the more often you do it, the better it is.

FREQUENCY OF INTERCOURSE PER MONTH

0	1–5	6–10	11–15	16–20	20+
2%	26%	32%	21%	11%	8%

Sexual frequency tends to decline with a woman's age and length of marriage, but not as much as folklore suggests. The main drop occurs after the first year, when couples have sex morning *or* noon *or* night instead of all three. For example, one fourth of the newly married wives said they have sex more than four times a week; that proportion drops to 12 percent of the women married one to four years, 7 percent of those married five to seven years, and 5 percent of those married eight years or longer. That was a happy and vocal 5 percent, by the way, eager to share their secrets of sexual success. From a wife married thirty-one years:

> We usually have intercourse and all the trimmings from four to five "settings" a week, and *always* on Sunday! By settings, I mean we rarely have intercourse only one time. We learned, before marriage, that you do not need to have an orgasm each time to enjoy it, that you can prolong the session and the sensations with practice. Everything is sex, from patting hands to intercourse. If you don't have at least two hours to play, wait until you do—don't rush.

From a wife married ten years:

> Only through patience, total honesty, communication and great love have we reached a good marriage. Our problems, and we have counted many, have helped to bring us closer together. We make love now more often—about five times a

week—than we did in the early days and we look forward to each sexual encounter so that we may learn more about one another.

In the past, researchers usually found that husbands wanted sex more often than their wives did—and, as a result, husbands tended to underestimate the frequency of intercourse while wives overestimated it. This posed a considerable problem in getting reliable numbers about frequency of intercourse. Husbands and wives often disagreed, which made researchers grumpy, to say nothing of the spouses. Kinsey felt that the *average* frequencies for each sex were valid and reliable, but other researchers began to distrust all self-reporting on the matter. (For example, many women come up with a monthly total by counting the number of sessions in the most recent week, and then multiplying times four. They forget that frequency drops during the menstrual week for at least half of all American women.) Researchers Richard Udry and Naomi Morris, however, did an experiment that suggests that women are more truthful than men in their estimates. Saying that they wanted to correlate sexual behavior with hormonal changes, they got daily urine specimens from fifty-eight women, along with their self-reports of sexual activity. When they analyzed the urine for traces of sperm, they found that the women's reports were highly accurate.

In the immediate case of the *Redbook* data, we are inclined to believe the self-reports. Not only are the majority of respondents satisfied with the frequency, but only a very few think they have sex too often, the traditional source of error in women's reports. Any error, in fact, would be in the direction of underestimation. One of the most remarkable findings from the *Redbook* study is the dramatic shift away from the "she won't let me" lament of the male and the "he's oversexed" complaint of the female. Today's marital dilemma is "he doesn't want to." In this study, 58 percent of the wives said the frequency of intercourse was "about right" —and most of them were the wives who were having sex very often. Only 4 percent thought the frequency was too high. *And almost four wives in ten—38 percent—felt they were not having sex often enough.*

We found very few women who have sex infrequently and who,

if they enjoy sex, are content. As one Canadian wife wrote, "I love my husband and we both enjoy our sex life immensely—when it happens [about three times a month]. My darling husband is not only puritanical when it comes to sex but also possesses a low sex drive." Her satisfaction with him is unusual. Most of the wives who have sex as infrequently as she does are unhappy about it:

> My husband neglects me in my sexual pleasures. I find it necessary to make my own pleasure or to fantasize. My dreams of life went down the drain a long time ago. My husband and I discuss this problem of sex often, very openly. It helps for a while—then back to the old three stars a month on our calendar. Yes! My husband gets a star for every time we have relations. About every three months I explode because I can't take it any more.

Of course, there are a few disgruntled wives at the other end of the sexual continuum. Too much terrible sex is not a big improvement over too little good sex, as this woman observed:

> My husband is very horny. He does not know what tender loving care could do for me. I have had to please him in bed three or four times a week since our marriage 17 years ago. He never cared how I felt. All he cares about is having sex. If I refuse him he goes into a rotten mood and won't have anything to do with me until I can perform "my duty."

With few exceptions, however, the relationship between frequency of sex and satisfaction with that frequency is clear: the more, the merrier. Of the women who have sex one to five times a month, three fourths say that is too infrequent. Of the women who have sex four times a *week* or more, about 90 percent say that is just right. *(See Table 8, next page.)*

Although frequency dips in the later years of marriage, satisfaction does not. Across all age groups, wives were equally likely to say they were having sex too often or not often enough. Perhaps as women get older their expectations—for themselves and for their husbands—diminish, and for some quality substitutes for quantity:

The frequency of intercourse was very high in the first six years of our marriage. Although we thought it very satisfactory at that time, we have since found it was only a slight opening of the door in the progress toward achieving our present level of satisfaction, ecstasy. The whole nature of the sexual act has shifted for us since those early frantic days. Now it brings a total giving of oneself in a way that was never possible then. Now I can satisfy my husband by being more openly, freely, and actively involved in the sex act. Although less frequent, our sexual relationship has led to much deeper levels of release, ecstasy, orgasm, feeling of togetherness, and love.

TABLE 8.

FREQUENCY OF INTERCOURSE BY SATISFACTION

Percent who say frequency is:	*Frequency of intercourse per month*					
	0	*1–5*	*6–10*	*11–15*	*16–20*	*21+*
About right	10%	22%	57%	80%	90%	84%
Too much	0	4	2	5	5	11
Too little	90	74	41	15	6	5

AGE AND EROTICISM

I had no sexual enjoyment until after menopause. My former husband was as virile sexually at 77 as when we were married 30 years before. My present husband is a wonderful lover. That is the trouble with the young ones, they have not learned the art of lovemaking which is really the best part of marriage. At 75 we are enjoying a sexual experience that young people of my generation missed out on. People seem to have the mistaken idea that one should cease to have sex because they are in their sixties or older. This is a fallacy!!!!!!!

This happy woman and her husband make love three or four times a week—long, slow, sensuous sessions. She shares certain attitudes and sexual standards with other women her age: She was a virgin when she married, never had an outside affair, never masturbates, and is private about her sex life—she talks only to her husband and an anonymous questionnaire. But she certainly enjoys sex.

Our society, which tends to associate sex and love with young people, and which regards aging as a disease rather than a normal process, has overlooked the topic of sex after sixty. The popular wisdom is that sex stops at menopause. Oh, an occasional older man provokes a national wink and a cheer or leer when he marries a young woman and fathers a child: Charlie Chaplin, Pablo Casals, Strom Thurmond. But since older women can't produce babies, and since fewer of them marry young men, we haven't as many visible signs of their sexual activity. But it is there.

Masters and Johnson, like Kinsey before them, found few biological boundaries to sexual responsiveness. "There is no time limit drawn by the advancing years to female sexuality," wrote Masters and Johnson. Both men and women may lose sexual desire over the years—the frequency of intercourse declines steadily for both sexes—but this is generally a result of lower expectations about sexual performance, boring sexual routines, or mid-life stresses. Sexual decline is not an inevitable result of the lessening capacities of the body. Many husbands complain that their wives lose interest in sex after menopause, and some *Redbook* wives complained that their husbands became impotent or uninterested in middle age, but these changes are usually socially caused, not hormonally programmed. "Presuming some continuity [of sexual expression]," said William Masters in an interview, "the only thing the male or female needs for effective sexual functioning is a reasonably good state of general health and an interested partner." To which Virginia Johnson amended: ". . . and an interesting partner."

The letters we received from older women certainly counter the stereotype of the sexless sixties:

> I am a widow of 62, and I go out with a young widower of 53. We make love almost every day and it is so fabulous! He

is only the second man I have ever slept with but I never knew it could be like this. Some of my friends think I'm a "dirty old woman" but my son says, "Mom, you do what makes you happy." My daughter can't imagine me with anyone but her father. I'm going to do what I want.

And from a sixty-eight-year-old mother of three, married thirty-five years:

> We live way out in the country, paradice lane I call it. I've never stepped out on my husband or he on me. This is such a nice place, running water all around, we made our own swimming pond. We love going naked all the time, we even work the garden, swim, saw wood naked. We both said we hoped this honeymoon would last forever and it is. We don't care what other people think. It's so much fun to put hay in the barn and lay down on it and fuck. We love saying words like that—they sound so important to us. We are always touching. I'm glad I'm not like Mama was—she slept down stairs, Daddy slept up, and they never give each other a good word. My husband loves fuckin good as I do. I cannot express the feelings I have now for this most wonderful place this side of Heaven. This is our summer love story and I hope fall winter spring will be even better.

With that attitude, it will.

Sociologist John Cuber has studied many types of marriages, and his essay on "the natural history of sex in marriage" offers an encouraging view of sex in the older years. Many couples, he says, "reestablish a quality, and even a quantity, of sexual expression which they were unable to sustain in their 40s." One woman told him: "We don't talk about it to anyone, but you're a professional and not so young either. We're over 60 and have as much fun in bed—or on the floor or on the grass—as we did before we married 40 years ago. Maybe one of the things that makes it all so precious, besides the great memories, is that growing awareness that we won't both be around forever, that the future gets shorter all the time."

The older women who wrote to us said plainly that the celebration of sexuality lasts as long as a person wants; there is no boundary year at which desire shuts off like a faucet. Sexuality, like love, lasts as long as life does. One delicious letter says it best:

> I am 60 years old and they say you never get too old to enjoy sex. I know, because once I asked my Grandma when you stop liking it and she was 80. She said, "Child, you'll have to ask someone older than me."

ORGASM AND AROUSAL

> The entire pleasure in a woman's body lies in the intensity of the pulsation just before the orgasm. Sometimes it is slow, one-two-three, three palpitations which then project a fiery and icy liquor through the body. If the palpitation is feeble, muted, the pleasure is like a gentler wave. The pocket seed of ecstasy bursts with more or less energy, when it is richest it touches every portion of the body, vibrating through every nerve and cell. If the palpitation is intense, the rhythm and beat of it is slower and the pleasure more lasting. Electric flesh-arrows, a second wave of pleasure falls over the first, a third which touches every nerve end, and now the third like an electric current traversing the body. A rainbow of color strikes the eyelids. A foam of music falls over the ears. It is the gong of the orgasm. There are times when a woman feels her body but lightly played on. Others when it reaches such a climax it seems it can never surpass. So many climaxes. . . .
>
> —ANAÏS NIN,
> *Diary*, Volume II

One reason that frequency and sexual satisfaction go together may be that more sex means more orgasmic sex: women who have intercourse at rare intervals generally do not reach orgasm on those occasions. Frequency of intercourse and likelihood of orgasm are more objective measures of sexual satisfaction than the catchall global evaluation of one's sex life. When one woman says her experiences are "highly pleasurable," her expectations and reactions may be entirely different from those of another woman who rates her sex life the same way.

A generation ago Kinsey startled the world by revealing, with a statistical onslaught, that women did have orgasms after all, and rather enjoyed them at that. In the first year of marriage 25 percent of his interviewees were totally nonorgasmic, but after a few years they got the knack; only 10 percent never reached orgasm during coitus in all the years of their marriage. Conversely, however, the number of women who said they *almost always* had orgasm during intercourse never hit the halfway mark; the proportion rose from 39 percent of the wives married less than a year to 47 percent of those married twenty years. The rest of the women reached orgasm now and then, hit-or-miss.

By the time of Morton Hunt's study, in 1972, a slight change could be observed. Over half of the married women, 53 percent, were orgasmic "all or almost all of the time"; a third reached orgasm about half to three fourths of the time; 8 percent said one fourth of the time; and only 7 percent said never. In the *Redbook* sample, the proportion of wives who have orgasm "all or most of the time" during intercourse had jumped to 63 percent, with the number of those who are nonorgasmic remaining at 7 percent.

PERCENT OF REDBOOK SAMPLE WHO REACH COITAL ORGASM

All the time	Most of the time	Sometimes	Once in a while	Never
15%	48%	19%	11%	7%

That low figure of 7 percent stands in marked contrast to the 30 percent of the wives who recall being nonorgasmic* before

---

*Many sex therapists dislike this word because it sounds too hopelessly permanent; they prefer "preorgasmic." It is, in fact, very easy to teach women who have never experienced orgasms how to do so, usually through masturbation therapy. Several books on the market offer step-by-step instructions on reaching orgasm through masturbation and then transferring those lessons to coitus. See *For Yourself: The Fulfillment of Female Sexuality*, by Lonnie Garfield Barbach (Doubleday & Co.); *Becoming Orgasmic: A Program of Sexual Growth for Women*, by Julia Heiman, Leslie LoPiccolo, and Joseph LoPiccolo (Prentice-Hall).

marriage. Apparently some women need the security and intimacy of marriage to relax sufficiently to enjoy sex fully. As noted in the previous chapter, premarital sex does not have much of an impact on marital sex or on happiness in marriage. But premarital sex does have one good effect, as Kinsey found: Women who are orgasmic before marriage are much more likely to be orgasmic afterward. The more often a woman reached orgasm during her premarital sex, the more often she has orgasms with her husband. In contrast, 80 percent of the wives who never reach orgasm now never did before marriage, either.

The more often a woman has orgasms, the more she likes her sex life; for example, 85 percent of the women who think their sex lives are terrific are orgasmic all or most of the time. This may not seem like news to you, but not so long ago researchers failed to find a connection between regularity of orgasm and satisfaction with sex. Several decades ago, many women neither expected orgasms nor sought them, and lots of wives never knew what they were anyway. Textbooks in gynecology actually recommended that wives indulge in some harmless "innocent simulations" of responsiveness to please their husbands; they would have been better off teaching husbands some innocent stimulations, instead. Everyone knew that women did not need orgasms for relief, the way men did. Thus many wives had low expectations of sexual pleasure, contenting themselves with warm, cuddly feelings of closeness rather than orgasmic ecstasies. They considered themselves lucky to get the warm cuddly feelings.

Naturally, if you don't know what you are missing, you don't know what you want. As one woman explained:

> I was married 13 years and sex was no more than a nuisance which eventually dwindled down to once a month. We never spoke about or read anything on sex. After 10 years of never having an orgasm, I finally got up the courage to ask my family doctor (they always tell you to ask the family doctor, right?), as my marriage was falling apart. His response was "70 percent of all women are frigid—it's all in your head." Years later I was divorced, started dating, but avoided sex like the plague.

Would you believe I was 36 years old before I found out there was such a thing as a clitoris! With the help of a considerate lover or two, and a doctor who took an interest in my welfare, I was encouraged to believe "there is no such thing as a frigid woman, only a poor lover."

Echoes of Papa Kinsey. Indeed, one of his most fascinating discoveries, which remained obscured by the voluminous data of his book, was that if women have trouble reaching orgasm, it is not because they are physiologically deficient but because of "the ineffectiveness of coital techniques." There is no built-in, biologically based difference in the speed of sexual arousal between men and women, he said. "The specific data," he wrote, "show that the average female is no slower in response than the average male when she is sufficiently stimulated and when she is not inhibited in her activity."

That was a real eye-opener in an era when marriage manuals were stuffed with advice to help husbands and wives cope with their assumed clash in sexual rhythm. Men were supposed to mute their rapid-fire arousal by thinking of the stock market or the China Question, while simultaneously providing the poor wife with enough "foreplay" to get her interested. Now here was Kinsey, saying that women become aroused and reach orgasm as fast as men do—during masturbation. If they are slower during intercourse, it is not because they are frigid, but because the men are too fast. In Kinsey's sample, some three fourths of all husbands ejaculated within two minutes of penetration, a finding that was the object of some terrible jokes in Europe, among men who pride themselves on their sexual sophistication. ("You want to make love?" "Adore it, darling, but haven't the time." "Not to worry, we'll do it American-style.") Kinsey thought that such speedy ejaculation was great for the preservation of the species, though clearly rotten for the preservation of the wife's happiness.

Today there are signs that the *Redbook* women and their husbands are not as far apart on matters of speed and timing as Kinsey's respondents were. Only a small proportion of the *Redbook* wives need a long time in order to become aroused at all, and most of them are apparently getting the variety and amount of petting and penetration they need to be orgasmic on most occasions.

The *Redbook* survey asked women how long it generally took them to become sexually aroused and how long intercourse must last before they reached orgasm. These questions are, unfortunately, limited and ambiguous. A woman may turn on very quickly but not want to have orgasm right away. Or on some occasions it may take three seconds to reach orgasm, but on other nights, in other moods, three thousand seconds won't be enough. "Achieving orgasm depends on the frame of mind you're in when you start," said one woman. "If I'm 'doing my duty' I may never achieve it, much less try." Another observed:

> Becoming aroused is often a very quick thing—sometimes only a few minutes—but extensive foreplay is necessary for me to reach an orgasm, which I have never reached during intercourse itself without continual manual multiple stimulation of my breasts and clitoris, along with intercourse. Therefore the time involved in [your] two questions is combined and often eternal. The only way I can reach orgasm in a short time (15 to 20 minutes) is with steady oral-genital stimulation, often accompanied with breast manipulation.

This wife is rare among the *Redbook* women, who report that they are highly responsive. Although the majority say they become sexually aroused within ten minutes of stimulation, the great majority need well over five minutes of penetration before reaching orgasm. But since so many say they usually do reach orgasm, we may infer that American husbands are not as quick on the trigger as they once were. Morton Hunt, who included men in his sample, agrees. Hunt discovered that Americans of all educational and occupational levels were taking longer in their lovemaking than was the case in Kinsey's time. "Prolonging the act is no longer an act of altruism, done only for the female's sake," he wrote, "but something done for the sake of both partners. Nowadays the goal is as much to maximize the enjoyment of the whole act as to reach its peak moment." What good news!

The proportions of American women who reach orgasm "always, sometimes, rarely, or never" depend on the kind of women

Average number of minutes needed	for arousal	for intercourse to orgasm
1–5	29%	28%
6–10	43	37
11–15	20	20
16–20	5	9
21–25	1	3
More than 25	2	3

being studied: volunteers? patients in therapy? gynecology patients? students? Because so many different samples have been selected, estimates of the number of totally nonorgasmic women in the whole population range from 10 percent to as high as 30 percent (except for those made by a few holdout gynecologists who think that all women are frigid). In contrast, estimates of the number of women who almost always reach orgasm in intercourse range from 30 percent to 75 percent. There is no way to settle this question to everyone's satisfaction, which is probably just as well. Some people will prefer to concentrate on the fact that a remarkably constant number of women still do not have orgasms at all, or only rarely, while others will be comforted to know that most women are orgasmic as often as they care to be.

Recently the female-orgasm question has been muddied—or clarified, depending on your point of view—by linguistic analyses of the meaning of orgasm "during intercourse." Should intercourse be taken literally—orgasms that occur during penetration (intromission)—or generally—orgasms that occur during a sexual episode, including manual or oral stimulation? The distinction is not trivial for the millions of women who are easily orgasmic by mouth, hand, and vibrator but for whom the penis is just a pleasant accompaniment to the blissful harmonies. Indeed, one of the central themes of *The Hite Report* was that a large majority of the respondents had difficulty reaching orgasm solely by penetration of the penis. Some of the *Redbook* readers agreed, noting that they had fine climaxes with manual or oral stimulation, not with intercourse per se.

I have conducted my own little survey and I do not have one friend or acquaintance who has ever had a "real" orgasm through intercourse—only through clitoral stimulation. However, try convincing a *man* you don't have orgasms his way. He won't believe you. But challenging him that way can get quite interesting!

I have never had an orgasm during sexual intercourse. To have an orgasm, I must have cunnilingus or manual clitoral stimulation. I know of women today who are faking orgasm during intercourse because they are too embarrassed to tell their husbands or lovers that no matter how long they keep their erection, they just can't make her have orgasm. *Please, please* discuss this when you print the results of your survey! You'll ease a lot of tension and make sex a lot better for thousands of women like me.

My husband and I have discovered that I can climax with a vibrator or if he performs cunnilingus on me, so most of the time I am satisfied with this. Once every year or so, I do have an orgasm during intercourse, and never can figure out what we were doing differently to bring it on.

I usually have an orgasm from oral sex, then another during intercourse. For a long time I felt abnormal and deficient because of this. Finally I realized that I enjoyed the orgasms which happened according to this pattern more than those which happened at the "right" time. It seemed silly to be trying to have my orgasms during intercourse just because other people liked theirs then. Foreplay, intercourse, and afterplay are all a part of lovemaking, so there should be no reason to make sharp distinctions about what happens when.

There should be no reason, but the controversy swirls on. One would think that the country's orgasm-insecurity rate ought to have been lowered somewhat by the research in the last two decades and the open talk prompted by the women's movement. The inescapable conclusions are that there is no correct or "normal" orgasm; there is no prescribed, official way to have orgasms, ordained in that Great Bedroom in the Sky; a liberated orgasm is any orgasm a woman likes. After all, there are many ways to get to Philadelphia. It should not matter how women have orgasms but whether they do. And the *Redbook* women do, with and without intercourse.

It was probably inevitable that after years of misinformation and ignorance about female sexuality, people would become obsessed with it. The woman's orgasm—and not just one, but several per session—has become the measure of sexual liberation for the wife and sexual competence for the husband. Now orgasm is like health: If you have it, you don't understand what everyone is fussing about, and if you don't have it, it is the only thing in the world that matters. When people are sexually healthy, the orgasm obsession should subside. It is not, after all, a major disaster if a woman—or a man—occasionally misses the golden O. As one wife said, "I sometimes have an orgasm, but it doesn't bother me if I do not. If I do—terrific. If I do not—no big deal. My husband does not feel rejected or unmanly if I do not. I never make a scene over not reaching a climax."

Other women are not so relaxed, nor are their husbands. "I climax on two of every three occasions," wrote one woman. "The problem is—now my husband expects me to climax each time, which puts a strain on me—and him. Do you think I should fake it?" The answer comes from a Nebraska housewife:

> Actually, since I've stopped worrying about all this, I've had more orgasms during intercourse, sometimes with no foreplay at all. When I thought I was abnormal, I never had any. Extraordinary.

Not so extraordinary, after all.

THE ACTIVE/PASSIVE DIMENSION: WHO TAKES THE LEAD?

> It's hard to say who initiates sex. Usually it doesn't actually *start*, it already *is*. It is so interrelated to our love that it is hard to find a beginning or an end—let alone who starts it! We are always touching each other. . . .

One of the best indications of the changing nature of female sexuality is women's increased ability to enjoy sex and their willingness to admit it. Women are no longer hewing to the traditional ideal of letting the man make the first move, and they are no longer lying in bed like ice cubes, waiting to melt. To be sure, most of them don't make their desires known by grabbing their husband's penis and shouting "Let's fuck!" and "Tally ho!" as they leapfrog into bed. But there are plenty of nonverbal ways of expressing sexual interest, and this group knows them all.

It is logical that the happiest couples are those in which both partners feel free to initiate sex from time to time, without playing roles of asker and askee. Women who say they initiate sex all the time, and those who never do, should be the least satisfied sexually. For instance, women who start all the sexual encounters often report that their husbands are passive, withdrawn, sexually uninterested:

> My husband is "too tired," "doesn't feel like it," "have to get up in the morning." It's awful. I have to make appointments with him for the weekend. He'll only make love after midnight. Boring, dull. Romantic, he's not. No wine, candles (he's afraid candles will set fire to the house).

Others never initiate sex because they are inhibited, embarrassed, or worried about offending their husbands. Or because they don't want more sex than they already have:

> I said I "sometimes" initiate sex—he doesn't give me a chance! Five times a week throughout my pregnancy was really *too* much. Even now I resent my husband's demands —if I say "no I'm tired" then he feels the rejection as being directed at him personally rather than at the act itself.

In this sample, just a small minority fell at the unhappy ends of the continuum; only 11 percent said they always or usually initiate sex and only 4 percent never do. Almost half (44 percent) do so half the time, and another 42 percent, more cautious, said sometimes. As we had assumed, the women who always take the initiative and those who never do were the least satisfied with their sex lives; nearly half of them rated their sex lives as poor. In contrast, 80 percent of the wives who initiate sex half the time are very happy with their sex lives, and only 5 percent are not.

Naturally, a woman who can tell her husband—whether by words or touch—that she is sexually turned on is not likely, during sex, to endure the activity passively. The *Redbook* women are as sexually expressive in bed as they are out of it. Three fourths of them "always or usually" take an active part in sex, and, again, they like their marriages and their sex lives far more than the passive wives do. But only 13 percent of this sample can truly be considered sexually passive. These women, who said they are "rarely or never" active during sex, tend to be wives who are angry at their husbands and who find sex repulsive or unsatisfying. One woman who said she is never active during the sex act explained why, all too graphically:

> The reason I am so down on sex is that my husband is the pushy type. He's only interested in getting his rocks off and doesn't really give a damn about the way I feel. He's so turned me off to sex, that it's just as bad as doing the dishes . . . he sort of made it a household chore. He rarely showers but seems to think nothing of begging me to perform fellatio. I could be turning green and gagging from the stench, but as long as he gets his way it's okay.

But the majority of these women would agree with the wife who wrote to say that she couldn't answer the question properly. "I can't say who initiates sex first," she said, "because our sex drive is amazingly parallel":

> We have times where we will have no sexual relations for two or three weeks and then have our own little orgy for a week. In addition, we have been willing to experiment, discard, and try something again months later so that our sex life today is even more exciting than when we were first married. All in all, sex is beautiful and I feel so sorry when I hear friends say they tolerate it. It's truly marriage's most beautiful way of communicating.

VARIETY, THE SPICE OF SEX

> I cannot imagine anyone having a more perfect relationship than my man and I have. I feel it is because he has encouraged me to experiment, without fear or ridicule.

> I read everything I can and do everything I can. If one saw me in the grocery store one would think me the all-American young housewife. And we all know that good women don't get off on porno (I do) or enjoy fellatio (I do) or (God forbid!) put her husband's sexual satisfaction before her children's getting a bath (they can wait).
> —*a mommy in Ohio*

When the mommies of Ohio become as sexually free and experimental as this one, we can be sure that sexual change really has swept through the country. The *Redbook* women are ready to try almost anything at least once—within the boundaries of a loving relationship. With love, the new sexual philosophy seems to be, almost anything goes:

- The great majority enjoy oral sex, both fellatio and cunnilingus.
- Almost half (43 percent) have tried anal sex at least once.
- Six wives in ten have gone to a pornographic movie (most with their husbands), and use erotic books, movies, and pictures as an occasional sexual turn-on.
- Almost seven wives in ten like to dress in erotic clothes to excite their husbands. Sexy lingerie and lace are the favorites, but three in ten think nudity is the best arouser. "Nude pleases him most," said one woman. "I still have all my pretty negligees from my wedding, 10 years ago."
- Three fourths of these women vary the location and setting of sex to make it more exciting ("Oh how I love the beaches and woods!" exclaimed one wife), and nearly two thirds think that the right time for sex is any time the mood hits.
- On the other hand, this crowd isn't much on sexual gadgets such as vibrators, oils, feathers, and dildos. Only 21 percent have used such devices for sexual stimulation—but almost every woman who tries them likes them.

The majority of the *Redbook* respondents drink liquor now and then, and 90 percent have had sex while under the influence. Although a much smaller group (21 percent) have had sex while stoned on marijuana, 63 percent of them said that the drug was sexually arousing, while only 38 percent of the women who had sex while high from alcohol said that it added to the sexual experience. Shakespeare's wonderful remark about the mischievous properties of liquor—"it provokes the desire, but it takes away the performance"—apparently applies to women as well as drunken porters.

TABLE 9.
EXPERIENCES WITH ALCOHOL AND MARIJUANA

	Percent having sex under influence of	
	Alcohol	*Marijuana*
Often	13%	5%
Occasionally	70	9
Once	7	6
Never	10	79
	Did drug contribute to good sexual experience?	
Yes	38%	63%
Sometimes	43	16
No	19	21

The *Redbook* women are not the sort who believe sex means a furtive disrobing in closets and a quick leap under the covers at midnight for a five-minute grope. Their only qualifier to the belief that sex is appropriate at any time and place the urge hits was a worry about children interrupting. "Any place would be appropriate for sex if we could count on being alone," wrote one woman. "With two kids around, being alone isn't always possible, except in the bedroom. That's inviolate." The children, we might add, can be of any age. One older couple said that their frequency of intercourse declined when their grown children moved in with them. A young woman summarized the general attitude about sex and privacy:

> What makes sex appropriate is not the day of the week or a certain room. To me love is warm and intimate—and when you feel intimate then any situation—car, boat, motel, bedroom, morning, night—fine! But on a table top at Macy's, forget it.

Few parents are willing to have sex spontaneously on the living-room sofa when little feet are likely to patter in. But, to our pleasure and surprise, the only effect of children is to send parents to the bedroom, not to sour them on sex. The survey found no pattern suggesting that having children lessens the frequency of intercourse or has a dampening effect on satisfaction with one's sex life. This does not mean that all women are unaffected sexually by having children; it simply means that for every woman who may be turned off to sex after childbirth, another is not. Children do not have a predictable effect on the quality of a couple's sex life. For example, some women did write that having children shut off their sex drive, especially if the children were unplanned and unwanted:

> My husband and I had a super relationship until the birth of our fourth and unplanned child. We love him but it has affected our sex life and I have lost most of my desire for sex.

But for other women, pregnancy and childbirth unleashed sexual passions*:

> For all three births I never waited the prescribed six weeks to have intercourse, but engaged in total sex about 7 to 10

---

*It was one of our frustrations with this survey that no questions were included about sexual feelings and experiences during pregnancy and after childbirth. For some reason, male researchers (and many females) just don't think of asking.

days after childbirth. I find that my sex drive is almost
stronger than it is usually—possibly feeling like I look good
again is the reason, though being pregnant does not bother
me. Right now I can't get enough of him—or enough orgasms!

Oral-genital Sex

Time was, not so long ago, when "oral sex" meant all talk, no
action. Cunnilingus and fellatio were considered loathsome perversions. Richard von Krafft-Ebing, who published his *Psychopathia Sexualis* in 1886, described a husband who abused his
wife with his "perverse impulse to commit cunnilingus." Although he allowed as how cunnilingus and fellatio are not invari-
ably psychopathological conditions, he was as subtle as a rhinoc-
eros in his judgment of them: "These horrible sexual acts seem to
be committed only by sensual men who have become satiated or
impotent from excessive indulgence in a normal way." The fact
that most of his case studies were murderers, rapists, child-abus-
ers, and sadists did not faze him in generalizing to what normal
people should and should not do. And his readers easily drew the
association between oral-genital sex and rape, murder, and
sadomasochism.

The belief that oral sex is a perversion is still enshrined in the
law books of most of our states. A typical provision reads: "Any
person participating in an act of copulating the mouth of one
person with the sexual organ of another is punishable by imprison-
ment in the state prison for not exceeding 15 years." If that law
were enforced, more American adults would be in jail than out of
it.

It took Kinsey, once again, to announce that oral-genital sex
was not merely the secret vice of a few weird and pathologically
disturbed individuals. Half of his sample of women had experienced both cunnilingus and fellatio, and about 60 percent of
the younger wives and college-educated women. They were not
merely enduring the "perverse impulses" of their husbands, either,
but enjoyed this sexual variation. "Many expert males," wrote
Kinsey, anticipating the advice of contemporary sex counselors,
"have learned to bring their wives to a number of orgasms in their

coitus [by manual or oral stimulation], before they allow themselves to ejaculate for the first time."

Today it is clear that if the sexual revolution has occurred anywhere, it is in the practice and acceptance of oral sex. Among people under age twenty-five, it is virtually a universal part of the sexual relationship. Hunt believes this change is of "major and historic proportions." By 1972, a majority of all Americans with a high-school education and a large majority of those with a college education were experimenting with fellatio and cunnilingus, and 90 percent of all wives under age twenty-five were doing so. Actually, if you really want to be impressed with the magnitude of the change, forget the numbers and take a look at the cartoons in *Playboy* over the last fifteen years. The cartoons have moved from jokes about intercourse, office parties, and illicit extramarital affairs to jokes about cunnilingus, fellatio, and group sex parties.

Given the national trend and confirmation from many other studies, the *Redbook* results are not astonishing. Basically, almost all of these women are doing it and liking it. Less than 10 percent have never tried cunnilingus or fellatio; the overwhelming majority like oral sex as an occasional or frequent part of lovemaking. Moreover, some of these women apparently think it is more blessed to receive than to give: More enjoy cunnilingus than enjoy fellatio (Table 10).

We expected to find that younger women were trying oral sex more often than older wives, but this assumption did not really hold up. Of the women over age forty, 16 percent had never tried cunnilingus, compared to only 7 percent of the rest of the sample —a statistically significant finding, but not a strong one. In fact, with so many women having experienced oral sex, we did not find many substantial differences between groups. The more religious a woman is, the less likely she is to engage in oral sex and to enjoy it. But that obvious statement is countered by the less obvious one that a hell of a lot of very religious women (87 percent) are indulging in what was once considered a sinful and shameful act.

Not only that. In this sample, the women who have cunnilingus and fellatio the most often, and who enjoy it the most, are those who are most likely to say their sex lives and their marriages are excellent. For example, of the women who do fellatio often, 42

TABLE 10.
PROPORTION OF WIVES WITH EXPERIENCE OF CUNNILINGUS
AND FELLATIO, AND REACTIONS

Frequency	Cunnilingus	Fellatio
Often	39%	40%
Occasionally	48	45
Once	6	6
Never	7	9
Reaction		
Very enjoyable	62%	34%
Somewhat enjoyable	28	38
No feelings	4	13
Unpleasant	4	12
Repulsive	2	3

percent rate their sex lives as very good, compared to only 23 percent of the wives who have never tried fellatio.

This is not to say that all women must practice oral sex to have good sex lives. Obviously, some are satisfied without it. One angry wife wrote, "Your findings upset me because you strongly led me to believe that unless we practiced oral sex we were abnormal." She said her sex life was fine, her (second) marriage happy, and she herself perfectly satisfied with "regular" sex.

But among the *Redbook* women, those who do not like oral sex tend to be women who find it a dirty and disgusting practice, whose husbands force it on them, or who are inhibited about sex generally. One young wife wrote:

My husband asks me to let him frequently but I shudder at the thought. This is an issue that causes arguments. My husband says that all women do it and like it. I say he's crazy.

This woman describes her sex life and her marriage as fair. She has sex once a week and almost never has an orgasm. She prefers sex to last just a few minutes so she can get it over with. Her dislike of oral sex is not an idiosyncrasy in an otherwise jolly and satisfying sex life; it is part of her general discomfort with all things sexual. That was the pattern in the *Redbook* sample as a whole: Willingness to experiment sexually was strongly related to greater sexual satisfaction. Conversely, feelings of repulsion about oral sex, either cunnilingus or fellatio, were related to sexual inhibitions and less satisfactory marital sex:

> It is all very distasteful. You sound like you approve of oral sex. If it is what I think it is! It's the most filthy, obscene, and unnatural. It can only be associated with a corrupt and decadent mind. The girls at the bridge club were saying how they had to hide the magazine from their teenage children.

> Anyone, including so-called doctors, that advocate or engage in oral-genital sex is unsure of whom or what they are. Oral-genital sex is abnormal and immoral. Believe me, everybody doesn't do it! Our mouths are for eating, drinking, speaking, and kissing those we love—not for using on someone's genitals.

> I feel that sex is something beautiful and good, but oral sex makes it seem dirty. Animals go around licking each other. Human beings are supposed to be more intelligent. Also, oral sex is unsanitary.

Well, 90,000 women can't be wrong. The assumption that oral sex is dirty reflects moral beliefs, not medical ones. As a matter of fact, the mouth is dirtier (has more bacteria) than the vagina or penis, which are entirely clean with regular hygiene.

The overwhelming proportion of respondents in this survey enjoy fellatio and cunnilingus as fun variations of sex, and it is undoubtedly their openness to experimentation and sexual expression—not oral sex per se—that contributes to their having better sex lives. Of course, there are some people who would launch a crusade on behalf of oral sex, if they could. To this woman, it is the remedy to all our social ills:

Women should not object to or feel disgusted by fellatio and cunnilingus. If two people are clean, as they should be for any sexual activity, those practices are as sanitary as sucking one's thumb or french kissing. Orgasms for both parties are usually as intense and pleasurable as coitus, sometimes more so. Of most importance, there is absolutely no fear of unwanted pregnancies; abortion can't exist. Oral procedures, if generally accepted and practiced worldwide, would solve the population explosion in a hurry. With that grave problem under control, hunger, starvation, and low standards of living could largely disappear.

Has anyone offered her solution to the United Nations?

Anal Sex

He watched the beautiful curving slope of her haunches. That fascinated him today. How it sloped with a rich down-slope to the heavy roundness of her buttocks! And in between, folded in secret warmth, the secret entrances! . . . he exquisitely stroked the rounded tail, till it seemed as if a slippery sort of fire came from it into his hands. And his fingertips touched the two secret openings to her body, time after time, with a soft little brush of fire. . . .

Though a little frightened, she let him have his way, and the reckless, shameless sensuality shook her to her foundations, stripped her to the very last, and made a different woman of her. . . .

Burning out the shames, the deepest, oldest shames, in the most secret places. It cost her an effort to let him have his way and his will of her. . . . Yet the passion licked round her, consuming, and when the sensual flame of it pressed through her bowels and breast, she really thought she was dying: yet a poignant, marvellous death.

She would have thought a woman would have died of shame. Instead of which, the shame died.

—D. H. LAWRENCE,
Lady Chatterley's Lover

Anal intercourse—the sin of sodomy. This practice has been so tabooed in Western cultures that researchers ignored it and even the lustiest writers merely alluded to it. Kinsey, who learned how to ask almost everyone virtually anything, did not report frequency of anal insertion among women, although he did discuss the physiology involved and noted that the anus was an erogenous zone for many people:

> The anus, like the entrance to the vagina, is richly supplied with nerves, but the rectum, like the depths of the vagina, is a tube which is poorly supplied with sensory nerves. However, the receiving partner, female or male, often reports that the deep penetration of the rectum may bring satisfaction which is, in many respects, comparable to that which may be obtained from a deep vaginal insertion. (page 581)

> The anal area is erotically responsive in some individuals. In others it appears to have no particular erotic significance even though it may be highly sensitive to tactile stimulation. As many as half or more of the population may find some degree of erotic satisfaction in anal stimulation, but good incidence data are not available. (page 585)

Kinsey concluded that psychological factors had a good deal to do with whether a person found anal stimulation or penetration erotic, neutral, or disgusting. In terms of physiology, the anal area is potentially erotic because of the nerve endings at the entrance of the anus, and because the anal sphincters may rhythmically contract during intercourse. "The anal and genital areas share some muscles in common," wrote Kinsey, "and the activity of either area may bring the other into action. Stimulation of the genitalia, both in the female and the male, may cause anal constrictions."

Today more and more women are discovering Lady Chatterley's experience with the "most secret entrance." The medical establishment is starting to recognize that some heterosexuals, not just male homosexuals, are trying anal intercourse, and discussions about the risks of and precautions for anal sex have found their way into the journals, such as *Medical Aspects of Human Sexuality.* "Entirely normal people engage in anal intercourse periodically, and many more try it as an experiment," writes Gordon Jensen, a physician and sex researcher. David Bolling, a gynecologist, reports that he consistently finds that some 25 percent of his patients—who he says represent a "broad sociocultural and socioeconomic basis"—have had anal sex, that they generally did not pursue the practice regularly, and that they had no long-term ill effects. These doctors seem to be in a minority. Most learned in medical school that anal penetration can cause all manner of problems, especially if the penis is large and inserted without lubrication, or if the woman submits not out of desire but at her lover's insistence (in which case she is likely to tighten the sphincters involuntarily and increase her chances of pain). But as gynecologist Selig Neubardt says in *Medical Aspects*, "I have examined many women who indulge in this activity, and have not been impressed with an unusual incidence of irritation or infection. I have learned not to trust everything I was taught in my residency."

Marlon Brando gave anal intercourse a shot in the arm, as it were, in *Last Tango in Paris*. The barriers have dropped, and people are talking more about this practice, even admitting to researchers that they are doing it. By the time of Hunt's study in 1972, some three fourths of his respondents, male and female, felt that heterosexual anal intercourse was acceptable. But most of them tolerated the idea more readily than they put it into practice. One fourth of the sample had tried anal sex at some time in their lives, and one fourth of the married couples under age twenty-five had done so in the preceding year. Of those who had tried it, most were not doing so often or even regularly. It was an occasional variation.

In the *Redbook* study, an astonishing 43 percent of the women had tried anal intercourse at least once, but only 2 percent do it often. Most of the wives tried it as an experiment and enjoyed it, but they do not enjoy it as much as they do oral sex. Only 10 percent of those who have done it said it was very enjoyable; not quite half thought it was unpleasant or even repulsive.

A number of women described their experiences and their reactions. Most had tried anal sex out of curiosity and love for

WOMEN WHO HAVE TRIED ANAL SEX

Frequency	Percent
Often	2
Occasionally	19
Once	22
Never	57
Reaction	
Very enjoyable	10
Somewhat enjoyable	31
No feelings	10
Unpleasant	42
Repulsive	7

their husbands, but didn't like it enough to make it a regular practice:

> Anal sex is painfully pleasurable but pain is not my thing, nor does my husband like hurting me.

> Anal intercourse is, for the most part, a strange pain/pleasure experience for me—cannot tell half the time whether it hurts or feels good. It is only particularly pleasurable when my system is empty and I am at the height of arousal before my husband enters.

Some who were trying anal sex were worrying about it:

> I really feel the so-called informed sexologists have played up this behavior. I consider this deviant behavior, just from the standpoint of health alone. It simply has to do with poor hygiene and cleanliness. We tried it a few times—what a hideous filthy way to go, what a way to promote urethral infections!

It is interesting that her concern about cleanliness is exactly the same worry that some women have about oral sex—the practice is dirty and promotes disease and infection. Nor have sexologists "played up" anal intercourse; they have simply observed and begun to study the increasing tendency of adults to try the experience.

We found a slight trend for younger wives to try anal sex: Of the women over age thirty-five, 39 percent have had anal intercourse, compared to 43 percent of those between twenty-five and thirty-four and 46 percent of those under twenty-five. The increase is small, but steady.

One strong finding, however, was that the women who are willing to experiment with anal sex are much more likely to rate their marital sex as very good than women who are not. The more often a woman has anal sex, and the more she finds it pleasurable, the happier she is with her sex life. These women are not simply enduring anal sex because of pressure from their husbands. They consider it a normal, if not frequent, aspect of their sex lives. As with oral sex, it is the uninhibited willingness to experiment, to explore all realms of sexuality, that makes for happy sex.

MASTURBATION

We couldn't get through this book without sneaking in a word or two on masturbation. It is the hot topic of the decade. The activity once thought to cause warts is now recommended to do all but cure them. Therapists advise masturbation to cure frigidity, teach women about their bodies, promote happy orgasms, express one's full sexual potential, learn about multiple climaxes, and survive sexually without a partner. Masturbation is the all-purpose tonic. And, as the wag said, you don't have to look your best.

It is true that masturbation training is the best, fastest, and most efficient way to teach women how to have orgasms. It is true that more women are realizing that masturbation is an important stage in sexual development and a normal sexual practice. It is true, as Shere Hite's book describes, that women will masturbate with everything from a zucchini to a washing machine, and derive pleasure therefrom.

It is not true that masturbation will replace good old-fashioned coupled coupling. To most women, it is not as much fun.

We are in danger of losing our perspective about the relative benefits of masturbation. Because so many women are recently discovering a pleasure that men have known about all along, many men are starting to wonder whether women will decide to chuck them out altogether. At the logical level, this is a foolish worry. Most women will prefer a man, with all his complexities, to a cucumber, vibrator, or washing machine, no matter how reliable those items are. But when it comes to sexual matters, few of us operate at a wholly logical level.

The *Redbook* women take a sane and refreshing approach. Two thirds of them have masturbated since marriage, and most regard masturbation as a normal activity—a way of relaxing tensions, an enjoyable addition to intercourse. But less than one third think masturbation is always satisfying; the majority masturbate when their husbands are absent or when coitus is unsatisfying. Indeed, the more often a woman masturbates, the less likely she is to think her marital sex is good and to be orgasmic during intercourse. For example, of the women who rate their sex lives as very good, only 10 percent masturbate often, compared to 36 percent of those whose sex lives are very poor. While many of these wives *occasionally* masturbate for the pleasure of that activity or as a way of sexual experiment, those who do so *often* are compensating for bad sex with their husbands, and they don't find masturbation especially gratifying.

The safest thing to say about these data is that they show that women aren't all that different from men. Both sexes masturbate, now and then. They enjoy it, now and then. They use it as a weapon or a release from frustrations, every so often; as one woman noted, "I masturbate only when I quarrel with my husband, and I don't know why, exactly—maybe it's to get back at him. Only he doesn't know it." They masturbate to tease and titillate their lovers, for fun. It's a once-in-a-while thing. No one thinks it's preferable to a warm-blooded partner. Surprise.

Since your marriage,
how often have you masturbated?

Often	16%
Occasionally	52
Once	7
Never	26

How satisfying was this experience?

Always satisfying	31%
Sometimes satisfying	49
Not satisfying	20

Reasons for masturbating[a]

Husband absent	38%
To relax tensions	31
Enjoyable addition to intercourse	31
Coitus unsatisfying	18
Sexual experimentation	16
Habit from before marriage	14
Husband enjoyed watching	9

[a]Respondents were not limited to one answer.

INGREDIENTS OF GOOD SEX, PART II: IT'S ALL IN YOUR MIND

Having spent all this space on the activities that make good sex better—frequency of intercourse and orgasm, willingness to initiate sex half the time, taking an active role sexually, experimenting with sexual variations such as oral and anal sex—we now turn to two psychological factors that make better sex best. These have less to do with what goes on in bed than what goes on in a person's head.

RELIGION AND SATISFACTION

The counsel that "it is better to marry than to burn" was not exactly a cheerful endorsement of sex. It was, rather, a grumpy acknowledgment that if a person could not stay celibate, well, he or she might avoid damnation by having sex in marriage—and only for procreative purposes, mind. Western religions instituted a long list of taboos and prohibitions on the sexual behavior of their members: no premarital sex, extramarital sex, masturbation, homosexuality, oral sex, sodomy (what *was* Gomorrah's sin?). No lusting in one's heart, either. The basic rule seemed to be: If it's too much fun, it's probably sinful.

The impression generated by sex research in this century is that very religious people are sexually inhibited, guilt-ridden, narrow-minded prudes who are afraid of their own sexual pleasure and intolerant of other people's. Many studies, as clinical psychologist David Ogren summarizes, found that the more religious a person was, the more restricted he was in sexual behavior and the less liberal his sexual attitudes were. Very religious people were also more likely to feel guilty over their sexual activities.

But the sexual revolution has hit the churches, too, like a thunderbolt. Kinsey located the first tremors. Religious women were less likely than nonreligious women to engage in nearly all types of sexual behavior *except marital coitus,* and, furthermore:

> While religious restraints had prevented many of the females as well as the males from ever engaging in certain types of sexual activity [for example, premarital sex and masturbation], or had delayed the time at which they became involved, the religious background had had a minimum effect upon the females after they had once begun such activities. (page 687)

In other words, once they got going, religious women were no different from nonreligious women, especially in marriage. Kinsey found that they had intercourse just as often, orgasm just as often (though it took Catholic brides a bit longer to become orgasmic after marriage), and experimented just as often. The only inhibitions that remained after marriage, if such they should be considered, were a reluctance to masturbate or have an extramarital affair.

This pattern of results is exactly what we found in the *Redbook* data, with one stunning addition: *The more religious a woman described herself as being, the happier she said she was with her sex life and her marriage.* This trend held for women of all ages—under twenty-five, twenty-five to thirty-five, over thirty-five: Strongly religious women said they were happier than moderately religious women, who in turn were happier than nonreligious women. (See Table 11.) The most religious women of all faiths were consistently more likely to report being happy most of the time, to describe their marriages and their sex lives as very good, to be satisfied with the frequency of intercourse, to discuss sex freely with their husbands—and even to be more orgasmic. This is not a portrait of religious prudery, by a long shot.

Remember that one cannot draw conclusions about all religious women in the country from these results. If religious women are more inhibited and sexually repressed than nonreligious women, they would be less likely to have filled out the questionnaire, leaving only those religious wives who are not sexually uptight to respond. So it is possible that these findings are an artifact of volunteer bias, and it is possible that there really is an important difference between religious and nonreligious women. In either case, the difference is worth exploring, because *within this sample* the two groups of women were equally motivated to reply and discuss their sex lives. (Remember too that the proportion of Protestants, Catholics, Jews, and atheists in the *Redbook* study is very close to the national figures.)

Why do religious women say they are more satisfied sexually than nonreligious women? Skeptics say the religious women don't know what they are missing, but in fact they aren't missing very much. Religious women are slightly more reluctant to masturbate, to experiment with oral and anal sex, and to use erotic gadgets or pornography for stimulation, but the lag between them and non-

TABLE 11.
DEGREE OF RELIGIOSITY BY HAPPINESS AND SEXUAL
SATISFACTION

Wives who:	Very religious	Moderately religious	Non-religious
Are happy most of time	67%	57%	52%
Say marital sex is good or very good	77	67	64
Say marriage overall is good or very good	88	81	76
Say frequency of sex is about right	62	59	54
Always discuss sex with husband	27	21	20
Are almost always orgasmic	72	63	62

religious women is not great. In fact, religious wives have sex *just as often* as nonreligious wives and are even more orgasmic, so their satisfaction is not just a matter of making do with what they have, or don't have.

Other skeptics say that these religious women aren't really happier, they just think they are happier. Or think they should say they are happy. This argument is impossible to contradict or confirm. As we mentioned at the beginning of the chapter, many people say they are satisfied when the objective conditions of their lives should make them miserable. On the other hand, who are we to tell another person how she really feels? Actually, if the objective elements of the religious women's sex lives were worse than those of the nonreligious women—if the devout wives were nonorgasmic, rigid about the proper times and places for sex, opposed to oral sex, wanted sex less often—then we could infer that their reported satisfaction was a result of psychological denial and compensation. But on most objective matters religious and nonreligious women do not differ. They are similar in education and income, too; their differences are not due to ignorance or starvation.

We think there are two reasons for the reported higher satisfaction of devout wives. The first has to do with expectations; the second, with changes in the churches themselves. Happiness is relative: It has less to do with what a person has than with what she expected to get. And it is based on comparisons with others: A person who thinks she is missing something is less happy than one who thinks she has found it. For example, in a survey on happiness for *Psychology Today,* which drew 52,000 replies, social psychologists Phillip Shaver and Jonathan Freedman found that many young people thought they were missing out on life's sexual opportunities. Everyone else, they thought, was having more sex and better sex (they were wrong). Everyone else, they assumed, was more satisfied than they (wrong again).

So perhaps the religious women in the *Redbook* sample feel happier than nonreligious women because their expectations are lower, circumscribed by a belief system that sets rules and limits. If your search for happiness is limited to a small patch of land—in this case, one marriage, one partner—you may be more likely to find it than if the world is your oyster. Perhaps happiness rests on testing what you have against what you seek, and religious women know what they seek, unlike women set free on an escalator of sexual sensation.

One woman agreed with this interpretation:

> I find it hard to believe that religious women have the appreciably more satisfying sex lives that you report! Probably they do not. But I believe that they sincerely believe that they do. Nonreligious women may be more objective because they aren't living up to a fantasized standard—they could have the exact same quality sex life as a nonreligious woman, who would be more realistic and objective about it.

It is hard to say who is being more "realistic" and "objective": the religious woman because she demands less, or the nonreligious woman because she expects more? For example, consider the situation of wives in their late thirties. Religious and nonreligious women have intercourse with the same frequency, a frequency that has declined somewhat since the first passionate years of their marriages. But religious women are more satisfied with that lower frequency. A third of them say they would like sex more often, but almost half of the nonreligious wives want sex more often. Sexual experience the same, satisfactions different. Who is better off?

But there is more evidence that the religious women in this sample are not lying about their sex lives. In the last decade, almost every major religion in America has reassessed its sexual philosophy. The advice that churchgoers are getting these days is not a sour "Do it if you must, but keep your eyes closed," but a rollicking "In marriage, anything goes; have fun, kids." The Reverend Leon Smith, director of Educational Ministries in Marriage for the United Methodist Church, recently reviewed some of the changes he sees in the churches' view of sex. The most fundamental, without doubt, is the new doctrine that sexuality is a positive gift of God, a happy activity designed for recreation as well as procreation. The official Methodist statement on sex, adopted in 1972, states: "We recognize that sexuality is a good gift of God and we believe persons may be fully human only when that gift is acknowledged and affirmed by themselves, the church and society." The Lutherans, two years earlier, had announced that "Sex, marriage and family are gifts of God in which to rejoice. Their essential goodness cannot be obscured by any crisis of our time." And the latest study of sexuality commissioned by the Catholic Theological Society of America defines a moral sexual act as one that is "self-liberating, other-enriching, honest, faithful, socially responsible, life-serving and joyous."

Obviously, religious people are doing a lot of rejoicing.

Smith indicated other trends in religion's new understanding of human sexuality: support for sex education in church and school; support and funding for sex research (a Methodist minister founded the National Sex Forum, which produces explicit erotic films for education and research); acceptance of homosexuality and masturbation as normal sexual variations, rather than perversions; and, most of all, a move away from rigid rules of sexual conduct. The churches are instead trying to establish broad ethical principles, Smith says, which allow individuals the freedom and responsibility to set their own sexual standards.

Smith's words are echoed in the writings of theologian Harvey

Cox, who distinguishes the spirit of religion from the letter of the law: "Law without Gospel," he observes, "is arbitrary and abstract. It cannot discriminate among cases . . . Evangelical ethics cease to be Law and once again become Gospel when the Word liberates people from cultural conventions and social pressures, when persons discover their sexuality as a delightful gift of God that links them in freedom and concern to their fellows."

There's that "delightful gift of God" again. The schism in religious teachings seems to be between those who preach Law and those who follow Gospel. Some listen to the old admonitions of what they shall not do, and others are heeding the new lessons of what they shall do. Both groups of people would consider themselves religious, but one is probably a good deal more sexually inhibited than the other.

More support for the changing sexual doctrine of religions comes from a study by David Ogren. Ogren wanted to know whether sexual guilt affects attitudes, behavior, and knowledge about sex. It does. In his survey of 207 college students, the men and women who felt most guilty about sex knew the least about it—their factual information was poor and their experience limited. That's not news. What was more interesting was Ogren's next step. He, and many others, had assumed that the more religious a person is, the more sexually guilty and inhibited he or she will be. Not so: Sexual guilt was strongly related to sexual problems, but religiosity (as measured by frequency of church attendance, present religious interest, and religious experience in childhood) was not. In other words, Ogren concludes, "religiosity per se isn't necessarily the villain in sexual dysfunctioning." Obviously some religious training can instill sexual guilt, but some religions do *not* produce guilt. Conversely, a child can grow up to feel perfectly guilty and have nary an ounce of religious training.

The letters from *Redbook* readers on the matter of religion and happiness are revealing. Some of the religious respondents were rigid in their morality, absolute about right and wrong—they are right, everyone else is wrong—and intolerant of any definition of religion other than their own:

> I feel that if anyone's gonna be a Christian, they may as well know right from wrong because that's what the Bible teaches

us. If you practice any sexual perversion, there's no way you can make it to Heaven. Those women who practiced premarital sex or believe it's okay are just phonies. Jesus warns *true* Christians to beware of phonies. I can see right through people like them. Don't let those women fool you by telling you they're Christian. They're not.

I base my sexual standards upon the only one, true basis— God's standards, which will never change. God intended sex to be fun and intimate and fulfilling between a man and a woman who are married. Only in this situation will God bless your sex life. I'm sick of hearing what other people are doing today, making those things prohibited by God [premarital, extramarital, oral sex] suddenly all right to do. Only by aligning your whole life according to God's standards as found in the Bible, will you find fulfillment.

But other women find pleasure in following the spirit of religion. They are not as ready to wear their religious beliefs as a suit of armor, to protect them against attack. Their beliefs seem more intrinsically motivated:

As women who have a close relationship to God, it is only natural to have a good relationship to one's husband if one seeks to do the will of God. God's word gives all the laws about marriage, including sexual satisfaction.

There is a difference between being religious and being a Christian. If all the women who answered your questionnaire would read Ephesians 5 in the Bible their sex problems could be handled at home. I think Sex is beautiful, I have been married 25 years, happily, and thank God, I can truthfully say [my husband] has been my one and only lover.

I place oral sex next to sodomy which is condemned in the Bible. It would be a different story if I were a frustrated Victorian woman, but I have been married 27 years with the same husband and we've had a beautiful relationship. You cannot attain sexual pleasure unless you make a commitment to God, to your husband, and maybe give more than you receive—but in the end you get back more than you give.

God knew what He was doing when he set up the 10 Commandments. Our home is based on His love through His son. Our love has grown through the years and is deeper and more intense than in the early years of our marriage. Not a day goes by that I don't thank God for making me one of the most fortunate women in the world.

There is only one definition of God in the Judeo-Christian scriptures and it is this: God is love. The sexual relationship is the deepest and most fulfilling culmination of the love experience. I was fascinated by your conclusions because it has long been my belief that the person most able to give and enjoy an emotionally satisfying relationship is the person who has learned to love in the spiritual sense. In this growing ability to love, we bring happiness to our mates, and thereby bring happiness to ourselves.

I was not surprised that strongly religious women reported enjoying sex. Our Scriptural heritage is richly sexual. My mother and grandmother, both deeply religious Catholics, were enthusiastic about sex and communicated this to their daughters.

I am 34, married 13 years, 4 kids, strongly religious. Both Old and New Testament say God began marriage, intending one man and one woman to love and respect each other, to cleave to each other. We are not only cleaving, we enjoy it! I do think life by the Manufacturer's Handbook is the most satisfying. As my husband once said, "Jesus makes the heart grow fonder."

We are both closer for what we have been through together and our freedom sexually with each other has been a nourishing force in time of sorrow. During long hospitalizations we have masturbated and during recovery we have mutually stimulated each other. I was really glad to see that your statistics showed that religious women enjoyed sex. So often my husband (who is a minister) and I have feared that the stuffy attitudes of some might preclude sexual pleasures for people in the church. I see no reason why this need be so. The Song of Solomon was a tribute to joyous sex and Paul advised mates not to refrain from sex with each other. I nearly always climax and after 20 years, we continue to enjoy each other sexually in every way.

These letters, and the statistical results, should help dispel the stereotype of the religious, narrow-minded prude. But religious people often feel defensive in this secular age, which may make them more determined to assure themselves and others that they are completely happy. We got no letters from nonreligious women describing the pleasures of having no religious ties. People rarely worry about what they aren't, just about what they are.

Once in a rare while we heard from a religious crackpot:

Sex is a snare and a delusion. Consider the unhappiness that has come to many as a result thereof. A very young man forced to marry too soon or burdened for years with child support, his life blighted because of sex. [Note she is not worried about the wife's blighted life!] Many in religious life have lived beautifully without sex. It originates in the mind.

But one of our favorite letters, from an older woman, illustrates what religion at its best can accomplish:

As I pass from early youth through middle age, and sail on happily past 70, *Redbook* grips me with velvet paws. I love it! Your report didn't hit on the chief reason for the tie-up between strong sexual happiness and a strongly religious nature: what we call God is basically *love.* We religious women care very little about religious authority, but we surely love people. We quietly try to reduce prejudice, and our husband's love is a great help in the constant fight against bigots. Your report didn't once refer directly to a husband's manual caresses as a prime source of wifely orgasms. They are invaluable after 40, in particular when a man has an orgasm only every 3 to 6 weeks (though pleasant daily erections). But when his wife needs a weekly release, he can give her an

orgasm by his heavenly caresses (both localized and all-over).
A husband with loving hands seems to his wife to be like God
himself in bed!

COMMUNICATION

> From my experience and that of many of my close friends,
> our husbands who are in the construction field do not need
> or want communication. They are bigoted, anti–women's lib,
> feel that the woman's place is in the home, in the kitchen with
> the kids.

> A happy, sexually fulfilled woman is a woman who is able to
> communicate with her husband. After 33 years of marriage
> I know that women require intimacy, the intimacy that leads
> to free expression. Too many men refuse to recognize this.
> Trouble in marriage comes from the refusal to recognize that
> partners grow and change over the years, from the lack of
> communication about emotional needs as well as physical
> ones.

Most sex therapists will tell you that it is relatively easy to fix a
sexual problem. But most sexual problems are not matters of
mechanics; they are failures of communication, and those are
tougher to solve. Many people do not learn how to express their
needs and feelings, even to their lovers, so resentment and misun-
derstanding build. In one study of 750 couples in conflict, the most
frequent complaint on the road to divorce was lack of communication, followed by "constant arguments" (which is the same thing),
unfulfilled emotional needs (which is the same thing), and sexual
dissatisfaction (caused by lack of communication and arguments).
   So it is no surprise that the strongest indicator of sexual and
marital satisfaction among the *Redbook* women was the ability to
express sexual feelings to their husbands. The more they talk, the
better they rate their sex lives, their marriages, and their overall
happiness. In fact, communicating about their sexual feelings is
just as important as acting on them. The women who never express their sexual feelings, and even those who do so only occa-

	Always	Often	Occasionally	Never
Percent who discuss sex with husband:				
	21	26	45	8
Percent in each frequency category who rate their sex lives as very good	56	43	21	9

sionally, are not the ones for whom everything is so perfect they have nothing to say. They seem to be the women who are suffering in silence.

The letters from women with good sex lives frequently mentioned that the questionnaire had provoked healthy discussion with their husbands:

> I went over this questionnaire with my husband and discussed each answer with him. It gave us a more open feeling about our relationship. Thank you for bringing these feelings to the surface. We have been married for 20 years and now have a much fuller and more satisfying sex life than we ever before thought possible.

> In answering the questions, I had to evaluate my own life and my relationship with my husband. I realized how much we had lost touch with. Thank you for the opportunity to face my own likes and dislikes—I think it will greatly benefit my sex life. My husband read the questions and my answers and found it very valuable. The questions made him look at himself, too.

> After we had discussed the [extramarital] questions and got my fantasies out in the open, he's certainly been more attentive lately, and we've had relations more often. I should have aired that one a lot sooner!

But the letters from women with sexual problems typically revealed trouble in communicating—not on their side, but their husbands'. One man wrote us with this opinion: "I think the greater degree of prudery and inhibition is found today among men, not women. Many men still feel guilt concerning their desires, conditioned as they are to believe that a man should be invulnerable and have no needs." There is much truth to his observation. It is ironic, in a way, that so much emphasis has been placed on female sexual problems, because, for all the traditional restrictions on female sexuality, women have always been expected and encouraged to express their feelings and emotions, and it is easier for most of them to seek help. Men, supposedly the sexually liberated sex, may face a much more difficult problem than learning how to have an orgasm: learning how to communicate their feelings. Listen to what these women say:

> My husband does not want help from anyone and resents my talking to anyone regarding these problems. I would like to share my joys and feelings with my husband, but he rejects them. Other women seem to have this problem to some degree. My husband is defensive, hostile, insecure in regard to his own sexuality but cannot admit that he has any negative feelings, let alone come to grips with them.

> My husband has no interest in anything. I have suggested the use of devices. No interest. I have attempted to encourage erotic conversation before and during intercourse, with no success whatsoever. Once or twice I had orgasm during intercourse but my husband spends no energy on duplicating these "successes."

> I am 42 and married for the second time. I recently realized that I have some sexual hang-ups and that I've missed the joy and fun of sex. One of my hang-ups, I know, is that I can't bring myself to discuss this with him freely. To my surprise, however, my husband has problems along that line. He seems to want to try anything and yet he is quite strait-laced when it comes to sex. He can't talk about turn-ons, either.

> I enjoy oral sex and experimenting very much. It's my husband who doesn't allow it. I answered that we never vary our settings for sex. That is because my husband feels the only place for sex is the bedroom, at night, with the lights out. I've

tried everything to get my husband to try a little variation, but he just won't have it. This questionnaire is based more on my husband's attitudes than mine. Even when I talk him into something new I can tell he's disapproving and that robs me of my sexual pleasure. He won't listen to me.

The most bitter letter came from a woman married twenty-seven years:

Most men say they want a really sexy wife, that is as long as they are the aggressor and do the asking. But let a little persistence on the part of the wife and what happens? A list of excuses that outdoes any a woman could make up. They seem to think they are doing their wives a big favor and what suits them should suit us. Why are men so dumb? When the man is impotent we're told we should be "understanding." Phooey! None of our husbands were understanding 20 years ago when the children were small and the demands on our energies were great. On the *two* occasions in my whole married life when I refused him, he flew out of the house and was gone for several hours. I always thought sex was great but in late years his technique and affection have gotten sloppy. Men spoil sex for themselves—they turn women off!

Without the ability to talk about changing needs, rhythms, and feelings, the relationship between a couple quickly disintegrates into the battle of the sexes this wife describes. In the *Redbook* sample, newlyweds said they talked about sex all the time, but wives over age thirty-five expressed their sexual feelings least often. Probably this is because they have settled into sexual habits and don't know how to renegotiate their sexual bargains. Possibly it is because they believe their husbands will be unresponsive to new suggestions. Whatever the reason for their increasing silence, custom does not breed contentment. The happiest women, of any age, are those who can share feelings with their husbands.

Sexual happiness, the *Redbook* women say loudly, rests partly on what you do and partly on what you think about what you do. A woman who makes love often, experiments freely, and is wholly uninhibited in bed has a happy sex life—but not so happy if she worries that other people have more and better sex than she does, if she feels she is missing something. A woman who is restricted in her sexual behavior may be perfectly satisfied, if she feels she has the best of all possible worlds. A good sex life, to modern American wives, consists of frequent sex with orgasm, a willingness to try new techniques and devices, an ability to communicate with their men. With those criteria, we can say that the great majority of the *Redbook* women do, in fact, have that miracle of modern society: a happy, sexy marriage.

What I like best about sexual activity is rather a combination of all choices—all our mutual activities and orgasm are made more pleasurable by the extreme amount of touching involved. Feeling the closeness of my husband, in every sense: spiritual, emotional, physical; the physical drowning in each other, and total overall caressing . . . there are not enough words for touch hunger fulfillment, but that is the ultimate in sexual activity for me.

One aspect that you didn't go into and that I seldom hear mentioned is that sex is so much fun! It is so many things— love, tenderness, satisfaction, physicalness, pleasure, joy. We feel that we have just begun to find out about each other's sexual being and to enjoy the wonderful life of giving and receiving in our relationship, of which sex plays a very important part, but still a *part* of our whole loving marriage.

4

EXTRAMARITAL SEX

I hear America swinging,

The carpenter with his wife or the mason's wife, or even the mason,

The mason's daughter in love with the boy next door, who is in love with the boy next door to him,

Everyone free, comrades in arms together, freely swinging,

The butcher singing as he wraps the meat diagonally on the wrapping paper, never straight, always diagonally,

Thinking as he wraps how he will swing with the fair customer come nightfall,

The school teacher, also now free and swinging, never lonely now, none thirsting for love, none a parched virgin ever,

Herself swinging in turn also with the choirmaster, with him singing as they swing and swinging as they sing,

All free in the great freedom that is to come, that is already here, I declare it as I celebrate it,

Every man taking unto himself a wife, no matter whose,

Every woman taking unto herself a husband, no matter whose,

This is my carol, my refrain, the refrain proclaiming none shall refrain,

None caring who does what to whom so long as it is done free and swinging,

All free, unbound and boundless in the new freedom, none stinting himself or another,

In the new freedom that is surely to come, is already here,

The great Freedom, the great Coming.
> —PETER DE VRIES (with apologies to
> Walt Whitman), "I Hear America Swinging"

He drew her further onwards, skirting a little pool where the duckweed made a carpet of green upon the water's surface. Dead water-lilies lay motionless among the reeds. At the sound of their footsteps frogs leaped hurriedly to cover.

"I am a wicked woman"—she said—"to listen to your words is madness."

"Why? . . . Emma . . . Emma . . ."

"Oh, Rodolphe!" murmured the young woman in a tone of lingering sweetness, and leaned upon his shoulder.

The cloth of her habit caught upon the velvet of his coat. She threw back her head, and her white throat fluttered in a sigh. She melted, and then, with tears streaming down her cheeks, with a little shudder and with averted eyes, she gave herself to him.

> —GUSTAVE FLAUBERT,
> *Madame Bovary*

Ah, those fictional affairs. Great panting passions. Life and lust renewed. Indecision and ecstasy, followed by the wages of sin: Guilt. Shame. Pregnancy. Death. Until the last half century, it was a rare fictional woman who escaped an adulterous affair with her life, much less her sanity. Kate Chopin's heroine in *The Awakening* (1899), torn between family duties and her devotion to her lover, resolves the conflict by walking into the ocean and not walking out. Endings like these served as stern warnings to those who were thinking of mucking about with family values. Besides, they often allowed the writer to finish the book neatly, without facing the messier truth: the heroine lived complicatedly ever after.

The time was when the only adultery that people discussed was the kind they read about. As Jane Howard recalls in *A Different Woman,* "During my high school years the parents of a couple of my friends were divorced, but those friends never, ever talked about it, and nobody else did, either . . . Monogamy, in our sheltered world, was the overwhelming norm. Not until years later did I hear the rumor that Mr. Baldwin, down the street, might not have died in his office, as we had been told, but in the arms of his paramour. Adultery, as far as we knew, only happened to people in books."

Today, extramarital sex is like the weather. Everybody talks about it, and few can predict it. It does what it wants to. It strikes at unexpected moments and to unexpected people. It happens to good old Uncle Fred, causing astonished murmurs to ripple through his family, and to pious Cousin Jane. It hits people who are happily married and those who are miserable, people who are not seeking it and those who are, people who think adultery is sinful and those who think adultery is a pleasant pastime for adults.

Extramarital sex was born with marriage; Adam undoubtedly fooled around with Lilith, free-wheeling hussy that she was, and it is certain that Eve's serpent wore pants and a leer. The gods always institute taboos where the greatest attractions lie, and every religion specifies whom one may (or, rather, may not) covet. Of course, cultures vary in their pursuit of monogamy; some wink at the notion of fidelity and others strive for it rigidly. In our own history, Hester Prynne won a scarlet letter for the same behavior that sent Elizabeth Taylor to the head of the class.

In recent years Americans have begun to discuss this aspect of sexuality as openly as any other, and the net impression is that everyone is doing everything with everybody. "I hear America swinging, . . ." sang Peter De Vries, "In the new freedom that is surely to come, is already here,/The great Freedom, the great Coming." But on closer inspection, we find that there is more fascinated talk about extramarital sex than action. In fact, it seems that many people would rather gossip about it than do it.

When asked their opinion, most Americans strongly disapprove of extramarital sex, or at least think they should. In Levitt and Klassen's nationwide probability sample of 3,018 adults (see Chapter Two), fully 86 percent said infidelity was almost always wrong, and only 2 percent thought it wasn't wrong at all. Although many people live with an obscure compromise between their ideals and their actions, in this realm of behavior as others, even extramarital action is not especially popular; the monogamous ideal lives and breathes. Of the women in the *Redbook* survey, fewer than three in ten had had extramarital sex, and most of those who did have affairs did not describe the stuff of fiction.

In short, the Great Freedom is not quite here. On the other hand, people aren't dying of adultery as often as they used to.

EXTRAMARITAL SEX: WHO, WHAT, WHERE, WHEN . . .

In 1953, Alfred Kinsey found the double standard to be healthy. About half of the men in his study, but only 26 percent of the women, had had an extramarital affair by age forty. That was the critical age; only a few people had their first affair in their forties or fifties. For women, the likelihood of having an affair reached its peak among wives in their late thirties. Kinsey observed:

> The younger married females had not so often engaged in extramarital coitus, partly because they were still very much interested in their husbands and partly because the young husbands were particularly jealous of their marital rights. Moreover, at that age both the male and the female were more often concerned over the morality of non-marital sexual relationships. In time, however, many of these factors had seemed less important, and the middle-aged and older females had become more inclined to accept extra-marital coitus. . . . (page 417)

The strongest inhibiting factor, as it always has been, was religion. Kinsey found that the lowest rates of extramarital sex occurred among the most devout women, whether Protestant, Catholic, or Jewish; the highest rates occurred among the nonreligious wives. Nevertheless, the wives were highly selective about their affairs. Of the wives having extramarital sex, 41 percent had only one lover and another 40 percent had only two to five lovers.

Some twenty years later, in 1972, Morton Hunt found little evidence of changes in people's attitudes about sex outside of marriage or in their experiences with it. The only news of significance was that the double standard was fast collapsing. "What has happened," wrote Hunt, "is that the males who will be unfaithful start being so earlier; as for the females, they apparently are on their way to catching up to the males in the incidence and earliness. But in the over-all picture, there is very little change thus far. The great majority of people still feel that love and sex are too closely interwoven to be separable at will or for fun." Furthermore, for all the chat lately about the "joys" and "freedoms" of sexually open marriages, most spouses are still grouchily possessive of their mates and do not willingly let them bounce into other beds.

In short, the absolute proportions of men and women who had had extramarital sex had not changed much between Kinsey's sample and Hunt's. The big shift occurred in couples under age twenty-five, especially for women: While only 9 percent of Kinsey's wives in that age group had had an outside affair, almost 25 percent of Hunt's young wives had done so. It seems that people who are going to do it don't wait as long as they used to. They must not be reading nineteenth-century novels.

Two years ago sociologists Robert Bell, Stanley Turner, and Lawrence Rosen distributed questionnaires to 2,262 married women of varying ages and educational levels. Their sample was *not* random, but biased in favor of better-educated working women; only a third were housewives, and the average age of the group was 34.5. Nevertheless, they found that same 26 percent who had had an extramarital affair, and most of these affairs were on a long-term basis rather than a one-night stand. Unlike Hunt, though, Bell and his colleagues predict a rate of increase for the current crop of thirty-year-olds. They think that some 40 percent of this age cohort will have an extramarital affair within the next decade.

The *Redbook* survey fits right into the current trends suggested by other research. Of all the wives, 29 percent had had extramarital sex.* As Hunt found, a good number of them are doing so earlier in their marriages. And, as almost everyone finds, age and length of marriage diminish one's reluctance to have extracurricular activities.

PROPORTION OF REDBOOK WIVES HAVING HAD EXTRAMARITAL SEX, BY AGE

Under 25	*25–29*	*30–34*	*35–39*	*40+*
20%	29%	30%	39%	40%

Length of marriage increases the chance of a wife's having an affair among housewives and employed wives alike, but the likelihood really jumps for women who have full-time jobs outside the home. Among wives in their late thirties, fully 53 percent of the employed women had had an affair, compared to only 24 percent of the housewives. One can't leap to the conclusion, though, that work per se turns women into sex-seekers. As sociologist John Gagnon observes, "the extramarital sex may have caused the going back to work, or the sex and the work may have been caused by some other common factor." We think the latter explanation is more plausible, because working wives over thirty-five were also more likely to have been married the longest and to have children of school age.

And work provides more chances to meet sexual partners than housewives have. Young mothers may not necessarily be more faithful; they may just have less opportunity. Some evidence for the opportunity theory is that the rates of extramarital sex for part-time workers and for housewives who do volunteer work fell exactly between the rates for full-time workers and full-time

*Hunt believes that Kinsey's figure of 26 percent was inflated because he combined married and remarried wives in his calculations, and it is known that remarried people have a much higher rate of extramarital sex—often with the person they left the first marriage for. In our sample, 28 percent of the wives in first marriages and 35 percent of the remarried wives had had extramarital sex, a small but statistically significant difference between them. However, the two groups did not differ on any other aspect of their extramarital experiences—number of partners, frequency, sexual variation—so we have combined them for the following discussion.

housewives. But from our conversations with women on both sides of the employment fence, we find a lot of opportunity-is-greener thinking. Housewives think that their employed sisters meet interesting, sexy men by the bushel. Employed wives contemplate the indolent leisure possibilities of staying home. Our editor, who juggles two young children, a husband, and a demanding job, eyed the statistics on the affairs of employed women with skepticism. "When do they get the *time*?" she wondered.

PERCENT OF EMPLOYED WIVES AND HOUSEWIVES HAVING EXTRAMARITAL SEX, BY AGE

	Full-time employed wives	*Housewives*
Under 25	21%	17%
25–34	40	23
35–39	53	24
40 and over	47	33

By far the strongest inhibiting force against extramarital sex is religion, as it was in Kinsey's study. Only 15 percent of the very religious women in this sample had done some serious coveting of their neighbor's husband, compared to 36 percent of the nonreligious wives. Religious affiliation itself didn't make a difference, but devoutness did. Of course, as we discussed in the context of premarital sex, a woman may change her religious attitudes once she has an illicit affair. As one wife wrote:

> My husband's reaction is the only thing that stops me [from having an affair]—he almost killed my lover one year ago. I live in western Kentucky, the "Bible Belt." I was raised in a strongly religious family and I have shared those convictions most of my life, but as you might guess I am having doubts about my religious feelings. This stems from my feelings about sex. Why, I don't understand, but I miss having another man in my life.

The most interesting result to us was how few of the women who have had extramarital affairs are following the example of literature, falling into a tumultuous, passionate romance that consumes their lives. On the contrary, half of the women who had had an outside affair did so with one man, and only a few times. Nor are they promiscuous, if by that we mean sex-seekers; less than 10 percent have had more than six extramarital partners. Most of the wives who had a lover or two seem to have done so on an experimental, tentative basis, and many would apparently agree with the woman who wrote: "I decided I got much better sex at home and have not been unfaithful for several years. Now if I'm attracted to another man I don't let my feelings show."

NUMBER OF LOVERS AND FREQUENCY OF EXTRAMARITAL RELATIONS, AMONG WIVES HAVING EXTRAMARITAL SEX

Number of partners		Number of times with each partner	
1	50%	1	18%
2–5	40	2–5	33
6–10	5	6–10	10
More than 10	5	More than 10	19
		Varied greatly from partner to partner	21

There is something to this woman's observation about better sex at home. Because so many of the extramaritally active women had had brief affairs with one man, most of them did not get around to trying the sexual variations they enjoyed with their husbands. For example, while only 7 percent of the whole sample had never tried cunnilingus or fellatio with their husbands, fully 40 percent of the adulterous wives had never experienced oral sex with their lovers. (And, as we know, this is a group that loves oral sex.) Conversely, 40 percent of the wives have oral sex often with their husbands; but of the wives having outside affairs, only 17 percent have oral sex often with their lovers. We are reminded of Erica Jong's observation, through Isadora's experience in *Fear of Flying,* that sometimes the anticipation of an affair is much better than its execution:

> In his room, I stripped naked in one minute flat and lay on the bed.
> "Pretty desperate, aren't you," he asked.
> "Yes."
> . . . Anyway, it was no good. Or not much. He was only at half-mast and he thrashed around wildly inside me hoping I wouldn't notice. I wound up with a tiny ripple of an orgasm and a very sore cunt. But somehow I was pleased. I'll be able to get free of him now, I thought; he isn't a good lay.

A one-night stand can be as exciting as a first parachute jump and also as scary. To say nothing of clumsy. This heresy directly counters the old Hollywood stereotype, in which movie lovers swoon magnificently into each other's arms without a twinge of first-time jitters. But the truth about sex in real life is that first times are usually more like a Woody Allen film than a William Holden.

Linda Wolfe, in her journalistic interviews on extramarital sex in *Playing Around,* found as we did that many if not most outside affairs are brief encounters, not lengthy passions. She talked with sixty-six middle- to upper-class women, and noted that the most common extramarital experiences were seize-the-day encounters, one-night stands, vacation adultery. Few of the women had long-term affairs. Wolfe concluded: "Even when an extramarital encounter had not been altogether pleasurable, many women tended to be pleased with themselves for having had the experience. In part this was because they felt daring. But it was also because they seemed to come away from their experiences reassured of the wisdom of their marital choices. The less pleasurable an extramarital encounter, the more a woman was convinced that her own marriage, even if it was rough going, represented a safe harbor." The tempting grapes turn sour, as the fox said.

EXTRAMARITAL SEX: . . . AND WHY

> What *was* it about marriage anyway? Even if you loved your
> husband, there came that inevitable year when fucking him
> turned as bland as Velveeta cheese: filling, fattening even, but
> no thrill to the tastebuds, no bittersweet edge, no danger. And
> you longed for an overripe Camembert, a rare goat cheese:
> luscious, creamy, cloven-hoofed.
>
> —ERICA JONG,
> *Fear of Flying*

Many theologians and psychiatrists would not accept Jong's
Velveeta-cheese theory of the affair. They assume that extramarital sex has deep and complicated motives which are to be rooted
out and obliterated. In this era of pop psychology, actually, the
moralizing of ministers (extramarital sex is a sin) has been re-
placed by the moralizing of some psychotherapists (extramarital
sex is a neurosis). But both kinds of analysis are often no more
than name-calling of people who behave in ways that threaten the
name-callers.

For example, consider the essay on female infidelity written by
psychiatrist Leon Salzman in 1972. Salzman warned that we must
not heed a woman's own explanation of her behavior; she is surely
rationalizing. One woman had had several lovers, and was perfectly comfortable with her marriage and her occasional affairs.
Her husband was not so comfortable and dragged her into therapy. There Salzman helped her see that "she could not justify [her
behavior] on rational grounds. She was able to see the elements
of compulsive greed and gluttony in her behavior. She reluctantly
discontinued her affairs."

Salzman would have been better off to discard his white coat
and don his religious mantle; clearly he felt this woman was
committing not only the sin of adultery, but also those of greed
and gluttony. But he is not through. Another patient had affairs
because her husband, she said, was not a good lover ("though he
was a successful professional man," Salzman adds in some amaze-
ment). Does Salzman teach the man how to make love? Does he
assign them some sexy books? Does he help them learn to communicate with each other? No. His diagnosis is that the woman is

suffering from galloping egocentricity: "She saw no discrepancy in the statement about loving her husband and also having a lover . . . Therapy was directed almost entirely to her grandiose attitudes."

Psychologizing, wrapped in a moral cloak, has filtered into everyday language and attributions for behavior. Monogamous couples often believe that adulterous spouses must be miserable, insecure, guilt-ridden, racked with remorse. One wife wrote that if adulterous individuals would only be honest with themselves, they would "be forced to admit that their actions were not the manifestation of a spontaneous act of love, but rather a compelling attempt to deal with their own personal insecurities." A husband wrote to explain why he had refused sexual temptations all the nineteen years of his married life: "I know from when I was single and making out like a bandit that the best sex is with the woman you really love." Now that is a lovely thought, but he is obliged to add that what is true for him must be true for everyone else: "Anyone who has an extramarital affair, no matter how successful they are in suppressing their conscience, no matter how much rationalizing they have done to justify their behavior, deep down on an unconscious level they know they are wrong and have been rotten to their partner."

The analysis is the same as Salzman's: Anyone who balances spouse and lover must be insecure, selfish, and mean. Look out for rationalizers, they say. No one seems to offer the corresponding warning: Look out for overinterpreters. The truth is that there are almost as many reasons for affairs as there are kinds of affairs, and it is foolish to try to lump them into categories of sick or sinful. The motive and opportunities for a one-night stand or a holiday spree are usually different from the motive and opportunities for a love affair that lasts many years. We found the whole range of extramarital experiences in this sample, and a long list of reasons for them. In the discussion that follows, you can judge for yourself whether the writers are honest in their accounts of their behavior or rationalizing away their neurotic needs.

The primary reason that women have affairs is also the most obvious. In study after study, the best predictor of whether or not a wife has an extramarital affair is her rating of her marriage. The better it is, in general and in bed, the less likely she is to play around. In Bell et al.'s study, for example, 55 percent of the women who considered their marriages fair to bad had had an affair, compared to 20 percent of the wives who were happily married (this 20 percent will be discussed in the next section). We found almost identical proportions in the *Redbook* survey: Fifty-one percent of the wives with fair-to-very-poor marriages had had extramarital sex, compared to 24 percent of the women in good marriages. However, one should keep the chicken-and-egg problem in mind here. Because we don't know how these women rated their marriages *before* they had an affair, it is also possible that having an affair makes the marriage less happy, or makes a woman aware of problems she has been covering up.

RATING OF MARRIAGE AND PERCENTAGE WHO HAD EXTRAMARITAL SEX

Marriage is

Very good	Good	Fair	Poor	Very poor
19%	30%	49%	54%	65%

NOTE: Bear in mind that the large majority of the respondents considered their marriages very good or good.

But from the many letters that came in, we infer that it is marital difficulty that sets women up for an affair. Some wives feel trapped in a hopeless, stagnant marriage:

> My husband and I do not enjoy a particularly good relationship, but he won't consider a divorce. We have never been able to communicate freely, and if I suggest something new in sexual activity, he immediately wants to know where and how I found out about it. He is jealous in the extreme and very rigid in his approach to life. As a result, I have had lovers before. My present lover is very special to me, and since I met him nearly a year ago, I have had no interest in other men. We are well matched mentally and sexually and have many more things in common than my husband and I

do. I have no feeling of guilt or wrong-doing. I have tried to end my marriage, but when one partner is violently opposed, the obstacles are endless. So I make the best of the situation.

Another common motive is sexual dissatisfaction at home. Although only a minority of the total sample reported that their marital sex lives were poor or very poor, they accounted for a majority of the women having sexual affairs outside of marriage. Some learned about sex and passion from their lovers after many years of fidelity:

> For 7 years I never had an orgasm with my husband. Until I became involved with another man I never really knew what sex was about. My lover introduced me to masturbation so now I can please myself when he's not here. And he showed me what real sex is like! My husband won't allow himself, or me, to really dig sex.

> With my husband of 17 years I'm supposed to be a good "missionary wife"—spread your legs and show no pleasure. Once every two weeks, five minutes and that's all. Thanks a lot. When my new love and I have sex, it can begin with a question or a look or a thought—and I am a full participant and we *fly!*

> I like my husband and basically we get along well, except for our sexual problems. I was 18 and he 26 when we married, and neither of us had had a sexual experience with anyone else. For eight years I didn't know there was anything better until I started an affair. I'm still seeing the same man after 10 years; he's a marvelous teacher. I've been completely uninhibited with him—enjoying every aspect of sex, foreplay through orgasm. My husband, after 19 years, is still inexperienced and bumbling. I simply cannot get aroused by him.

Of course, for some women sexual problems are merely the tip of the iceberg. One wife began a letter explaining that she had affairs because sex with her husband was not enjoyable. But before long she revealed that her sexual experimentation was also a means of attaining independence and self-esteem:

> I have been married 24½ years and sexually it has been ZERO for years. Not because I don't want sex but because I don't want it with my husband. He is very routine, unexperimental, frustrating and unsatisfying. I don't hate him, but we are very different in emotion and personality. Until a few years ago I had accepted the unsatisfying life in marriage but now I have decided to explore for myself. I have served this family all those years, and though my husband has had my best years to date, there are many best years to be. I will be 50 soon but don't appear to be my age. I feel young and I love life. I have had two serious affairs plus one casual affair. At present I am interested in one man and have been having a steady affair for 11 months. This man is the best lover I ever had. We have considered marriage seriously but I need to find my independent position first.

Of the wives who rate their marital sex lives as very good, only 18 percent (in Bell et al.'s study) and 22 percent (in ours) had had extramarital sex; in contrast, about half of the women with poor or very poor sex lives had lovers. For some of these dissatisfied wives, the sexual problem was merely a low frequency: They felt they weren't having sex often enough at home, so they sought it elsewhere. But an equal number thought their marital sex was *too frequent*—undoubtedly, we think, because they prefer sex with their lovers to sex with their husbands, and thus regard their husbands' overtures as unwelcome. *(See Table 12.)*

To gather data for his book *The Affair,* Morton Hunt sent questionnaires to 360 middle-class Americans and interviewed 80 adulterous adults. Again, not a random sample, but his conclusions agree with other research. Love, he concluded, "is actually rather uncommon as a cause of infidelity." Among his interviewees, only one wife in five (and one husband in ten) said that falling in love was the primary cause of their first affair. This finding is especially remarkable for a society that considers love and romance virtually the only circumstances that justify extramarital sex. But Hunt thinks the main motivation was boredom, pure and simple. "Among my interviewees," he wrote, "well

TABLE 12.

EVALUATION OF SEX IN MARRIAGE AND PERCENT HAVING
EXTRAMARITAL SEX

Percent of women in each category having extramarital sex	Bell, Turner, and Rosen (1975)	Redbook (1974)
Rate sexual aspect of marriage as very good	18	22
Rate marital sex poor or very poor	48	48
Think frequency of sex in marriage is about right	21	24
Think marital sex too frequent	38	44
Think marital sex too infrequent	34	34
Rate marriage overall as good or very good	20	24
Rate marriage as fair to very poor	55	51

over half the men admitted that one kind of boredom or another was the major reason for their first affairs; so did an even larger number of women, almost two thirds of whom blamed the emotional boredom of marriage." The sister motive was self-esteem: Affairs made Hunt's interviewees feel good, flattered, and sexy.

One monogamous wife wrote her opinion of women who have affairs out of such needs. They share one trait, she said: immaturity. "I would consider the idea of these women needing the attentions of new bed mates to reassure their egos, vanities, etc. They do not give me the image of the new liberated woman but rather they have succumbed to that age-old need to be flattered, desired, etc. before they can feel like a woman." Some respondents acknowledged these motives:

With my lover I know I am adored and loved and appreciated and I feel like the most beautiful woman in the world!

I had my love affair because of loneliness. My husband never talks or tells me I look nice. I guess it all happens because of ego and to see if another man can fulfill these needs. I loved my lover and always will, but because of my children I wouldn't leave.

I think half my problem with my husband is because he is not affectionate. Married 10 years and no kisses, no hugs, not even a pinch on the fanny. He never says "I love you"—he says I'm supposed to know that.

Self-esteem is not a trivial motive for behavior. Feeling good and feeling appreciated are powerful sensations. But some women in our sample were having affairs for stronger reasons than a desire for hugs and affection or mid-week energizers. For them, extramarital sex gave them nothing less than life, awakening them to possibilities that had been dormant:

I'm 37, 3 children, married 16 years. I have had one affair since I've been married. This one man means more to me than anyone in this world (other than my kids). Neither one of us would leave our spouses. He's my dentist—not all things you hear about dentists are true. He makes me want to live. I never cared what I did, how I looked, or really didn't think much about life til he came along. If nothing more comes of this relationship, I'm thankful he touched my life.

My lover sees me as a different person, and because of this I have grown and am now trying to attain goals I had never thought possible. This fall, after 18 years of marriage, I returned to college to take classes in computer science.

Perhaps the most poignant contrast between a wife's reality with her husband and a romance with her lover came from this sad woman:

To me the sex act should be a beautiful act between two people who really love each other. My husband used sex to barter with; if I gave it to him, I got money for groceries; if I didn't, no money. That is God's truth. It looks so awful in print. Once I went to the hospital for minor surgery; I wasn't really scared, just a little anxious, and wanted a little sympathy the night before. He wanted sex, and didn't get it, and so he didn't come to see me in the hospital.

Once I had a lover. We actually didn't have much sex, but what we did have was satisfying and fulfilling. I saw him for four years. He loved me for myself. A lot of times we enjoyed just being together; he liked my company, I liked his. It was the first affair for him, the first for me; we felt guilty, yet we couldn't stop ourselves. I felt sure that if we ever did get married he would continue to treat me as before, and not change as my husband had. Then, suddenly, God took him from me. But, illicit or not, I thank God for those four years, they showed me what it was like to live with a man who loved you for yourself.

So long as people have affairs, there will be other people who try to sort them into categories and probe their motives. Hunt ranks extramarital dalliance into four types, from low-involvement, casual conquests that reaffirm one's desirability to "affairs of fulfillment," all-encompassing love affairs. In between, he says, are affairs of moderate involvement, intended to supplement something missing from the marriage, and affairs of rebellion, in which the spouse is rebelling against the demands of adulthood and responsibility. Most people fall at the lower ends of this continuum, and rarely get the Lady Chatterley affair that breaks up the marriage. Contrary to myth, Hunt adds, most of his interviewees felt no strong passions either before or after their affairs, felt little guilt, and stayed married, with no disastrous consequences.

Although the *Redbook* survey did not inquire about motives or consequences of extramarital sex, the comments and letters we received supported Hunt's view. Most of the women who felt guilty were those who were *thinking* of having an affair:

My husband is sexually uptight. I could probably have an extramarital affair anytime I want to. I've come close to it sometimes, and where I work all I have to do is look at a guy a certain way, and he will know I'm ready. But I think it may hurt my marriage right now. I would feel too guilty.

Once a woman starts an affair, guilt subsides. As Salzman would say, her ability to rationalize takes over:

Occasionally, the guilt feelings come. Sometimes I feel guilty because I am being an unfaithful wife; other times I feel guilty because I feel I am keeping my lover from finding a woman he could love and marry and have completely to himself. But when we talk these things out we realize we don't want to give up this happiness we have found with each other.

Another woman gave up an affair, not because she felt guilty but because she thought she would be found out:

Although adultery is morally wrong and a sin, it taught me much about my own feelings and my relationship with my spouse. At 42, after having an affair with one man for four years, I finally decided I had to give him up or give up my good husband and disgrace my three wonderful grown children. The lying and cheating were so easy, but I was getting so used to it I was afraid I'd slip and be found out. A day doesn't go by but what I'm reminded in some way of my past with my love and it isn't easy. If I had it to do over I *never* would have done it. Thanks to God my husband never knew.

But one woman cut straight through the self-analysis, rationalizations, explanations, convolutions, and theories:

Why did I have my first affair after 33 years of marriage? I could give you pages of reasons, but the real one is: It's fun! It's fun and exciting! If I had not had this affair I would have become a frustrated old lady! All my life I have done what others expected of me. Now I feel I am the ruler of my own body, and it makes me feel good to have the courage to fulfill my desires.

THE 6-PERCENT SOLUTION

We said earlier that most women who are involved in affairs fall into them because of marriage complaints; the marriage may be merely boring, or it may have become a battlefield of miscommunication and sexual incompatibility. But of the women who have extramarital sex (keep in mind that that is only 29 percent of all the respondents), a sturdy minority, 20 percent, say they are happily married. These women confound the researchers and therapists who can't believe that wives can do what many husbands have done for centuries, enjoy both spouse and lover. Women are supposed to be monogamous, right?

To be sure, the women who are happily married and have a simultaneous happy love affair are a small proportion of the whole sample, only 6 percent. But they recur in many studies, large and small, a consistent 6 percent of all wives or 20 percent of the wives who have had extramarital sex. Indeed, the similarity between Bell et al.'s sample and ours is striking (see Table 12). According to these women, their marriages are good, their sex lives with their husbands are good, and they are totally satisfied with the frequency of marital sex, which tends, incidentally, to be higher than average. They are able to discuss their sexual feelings and desires with their husbands, take an active role sexually, and enjoy all sorts of sexual variations. *But* they also have lovers.

Some women in the 6 percent love their husbands and have occasional affairs that do not affect their marriages. As one older wife explained, "I think I feel younger than my years because of my interest in other men":

> Although I have a good husband and our sex life is satisfactory, I engage in extramarital activity. I was 48 years old and had been married 26 years before I experienced sex outside of marriage. That affair was with a man I met at work who was very experienced and who taught me much about sexual enjoyment. My husband knows nothing of my experiences and I hope to keep it that way, although there is always the danger of being found out. I attend church regularly but don't consider myself especially religious.

But most of the women in this category are not dallying for the sake of feeling youthful. Most have one lover whom they have been seeing for years, who has become virtually a second husband. These women have significantly fewer lovers than wives who are unhappily married.

SATISFACTION WITH MARRIAGE AND NUMBER OF EXTRAMARITAL PARTNERS, AMONG WOMEN HAVING EXTRAMARITAL AFFAIRS

Number of lovers	Happily married	Unhappily married
1	54%	43%
2–5	38	43
6–10	4	6
More than 10	4	7

Many letters came from women who wanted to describe their lives with "two husbands":

> I feel that I can love my husband and be a good wife and mother to our two children *and still* have sex with and even emotionally care for another man at the same time.

> I'm more fortunate than most in that I do get to meet my lover on a continuing, if irregular basis. We are both married, have the same number of children, and our two families are friends. I feel that I have the best of several worlds really. How long do affairs last? I don't know what lies ahead, but this loving, supporting relationship has passed the nine-year mark.

> My extramarital relationship is sexually exciting and an emotional supplement to my marriage. My lover and I have been together 4½ years so far.

> I'm 31, married 10½ wonderful years, 2 children, and a six-year relationship with a lover. A woman who goes from

man to man (judging from the women I've known) does so to get caught and does *not* have a satisfying marriage. My husband doesn't know about my affair, and it takes nothing from my marriage. All I know is that I do love them both and my life would be incomplete without one of them. I could never live with my lover—we're too alike—but I hope it lasts forever.

Some women seem totally surprised at their own ability to combine husband and lover, contrasting their community image with their internal feelings:

> I am 32, 4 lovely children, happily married, very good marital sex, satisfied with the frequency (12–13 times a month), very happy with life—and having extramarital sex. Why? Why are there 20 of us out of a 100 who have had extramarital sex? I thought I was one in a thousand until I read your survey! I am considered the home-maker type—dress well, 4-H leader, hold a part-time job, am well liked in the community, keep a lovely home, sew, bake everything from scratch. So here I am, the envy of many women, and I'm having extramarital sex!

Several women wrote lengthy accounts of their two relationships, trying to explain what each offered them. One wife unwittingly confirmed two of Balzac's wonderful maxims: "A lover has all the virtues, and all the defects, that a husband has not"; "It is easier to be a lover than a husband, for the same reason that it is more difficult to show a ready wit all day long than to say a good thing occasionally." She got passion and romance with her lover and calm stability with her husband:

> Here I am, a wife with a happy marriage, a mother of three beautiful children, a career woman taking college courses at night—and having an affair for the past five years with the same man. I cannot really talk to my husband but with my lover I am completely open and honest. My husband forgets my birthday, our anniversary, Mother's Day, in short, everything except Christmas. My lover is a sentimentalist who

would remember Ground Hog Day if it meant something special to us.

I love them both but in different ways—one because of the happy times and the struggles and problems we've shared in our marriage, and the other for some of the same reasons plus many which are deeper. What we share is something people are fortunate to find once in a lifetime. Sex is not the most important thing in the world; the feeling of utter oneness with another person, in thoughts and actions in all aspects of life, means far more to me than sex. Yet when I have all these things, sex adds another dimension to my fulfillment as a woman.

But there are plenty of sentimental, attentive, loving husbands whose wives have affairs anyway, for other reasons. One woman, who described herself as very religious, very "anti–women's lib," wrote:

I am happily married to a man I love, respect, and am proud of. We have gotten along well for 18 years. I am 38 years old. However two years ago I began having a relationship with another man. It led to love and intercourse. I don't know why because my husband has always been very affectionate and attentive to me in all respects. Even when he is out of town he always calls. I just found myself strongly attracted to this male friend. We get along well in every respect, not just sexually. I feel married to two men.

Actually, this respectable mother of seven does know perfectly well why she took a lover:

My lover fills a need that my husband can not. My lover has more time to just concentrate on me. I basically am not a selfish person but I find I *thoroughly* enjoy the *complete* attention I receive from this man.

Balzac would have smiled.

Some older women, after many years of marriage, find themselves in the predicament of loving their husbands but not being in love with them. They want to stay married, perhaps because of the affectionate bond of years together, perhaps because they fear to strike off on their own, but they find a lover to provide a sense of growth, change, and excitement.

> I am 52, married 33 years, fairly religious, active in civic and church affairs. We are in the lower middle-income group and live in a fairly large southeastern city. Our world and society have changed in the past ten years—I have adapted because I like most of the changes; my husband does not. I still think our marriage is good, but if society had accepted trial marriages 33 years ago I probably would not have stayed with him. Now I would feel very insecure about leaving him and trying to make a living for myself. The man I am having an affair with and I have weighed the risk of continuing our relationship. From the beginning, six years ago, we had no intentions of breaking up each other's marriage. We found in each other an exciting, compassionate relationship that neither of us had known with our respective mates.

We were impressed by the number of wives who described love affairs of long duration—three, six, nine, ten years. The myth, after all, is that the husband soon finds out and shoots the wife and/or the lover, or shouts "A plague on both your houses!" and departs for the divorce court. Or that the husband doesn't find out and the wife wallows in guilt and indecision and gives up the lover, or wallows in guilt and indecision and gives up the husband. In fact, many of these women did not seem to feel guilty at all and were not especially motivated to give up either partner. If they were indecisive, it was because they felt no need to make a decision. Nevertheless, the compromises are not always pain-free:

> It made me sad that some of my answers seem a harsh judgment on my husband of almost 18 years, and the father of our four children. We have been through many good things together. We are good friends, enjoy one another's company, and I still love him, though I am no longer turned on by him. He still seems very turned on to me and would enjoy sex every other night if not oftener. Grinding poverty has destroyed the

good sex life we once enjoyed. I keep hoping that once again
I'll find that I am in love and turned on by my husband. This
is a feeling that I found many women feel, but are afraid to
voice because it makes them feel unloyal. In the meantime I
am able to find sexual and emotional fulfillment with my
lover. Our relationship has been going on for over 3 years. He
is single and 9 years my junior. My husband knows my lover
and knows of our affair, but he would rather that I have an
affair than break up our marriage in search of sexual fulfillment.

The singular characteristic of this group is that their love affairs
are marked as much by love as by lust. We turn now to an even
smaller minority: those women who enjoy extramarital sex as
recreation.

SWINGERS AND SWAPPERS

Mate-swapping and other organized versions of extramarital
sex caught the media eye a decade ago. Remember how fascinated
and horrified people were to read about key clubs (or key parties),
in which suburban couples tossed their house keys into a pot and
each selected a neighbor's key and spouse for an evening of unpre-
dictable sport? Remember the Sexual Freedom League and its
organized orgies? Remember the sexist days when mate-swapping
was called "wife-swapping," which in fact accurately described
which spouse was initiating the activity?
Media reports have diminished since the heyday of group sex,
but social scientists still venture where reporters are tired of tread-
ing. Some sociologists have even sacrificed themselves to the experience, joining in for the sake of science. Others ask questions from
a safe distance. What they have learned is that group sex, swinging, and swapping are exceedingly rare on the American sex scene
—in spite of all the cartoons, jokes, studies, and the big-city under-
ground of newsletters and networks that get swinging couples
together.
In his 1971 book *Group Sex,* anthropologist Gilbert Bartell
ventured the guess that at most 1 percent of all married couples

had tried swinging (exchanging partners with another couple). In Hunt's 1972 study, less than 2 percent had done so, many of them only once. Hunt commented that "those who practice mate-swapping with frequency or regularity are too few in number to justify precise percentaging, and amount to tiny fractions of 1 percent of our married males and females."

The *Redbook* sample fits this picture. Readers were asked: "Have you ever engaged in mate-swapping, where you and your husband exchanged partners with another couple for the purpose of having sexual relations?" Only 0.5 percent said they do so often; 1.2 percent had exchanged partners on occasion; and 2 percent had tried swinging just once. On the other hand, a goodly number who have *not* swapped mates are fantasizing about doing it. When the nonswinging wives were asked whether they "would like to do so at some time in the future," only 76 percent said definitely not. However, only 2 percent said definitely yes. The rest were undecided: Five percent said "perhaps," and 17 percent said "I'm not sure," which sounds suspiciously like "perhaps." Of course, since fantasies and reality have a tenuous connection at best, we can't say what these uncertain wives would actually do if opportunity appeared in their living rooms.

We found no generational trend of increased willingness to experiment with swinging. The same proportion of wives who had swapped partners at least once (4 percent) turned up in every age group—the under-twenties, twenties, thirties, and over-forties. What we may be dealing with in this small number of women, in short, is not a new phenomenon but an old fact. There is some evidence that swinging wives are simply women with especially high and uninhibited sex drives. They are most likely to enjoy all sexual activities, to practice oral and anal sex often with their husbands, to have their first intercourse at an early age, to have had and enjoyed sexual experiences with another woman.

One thirty-year-old wife, married eight years and the mother of a two-year-old son, best represents this group. She grew up in a small Southern community and was very religious, but left town and religion when she moved to the big city. Her husband, she says, is "one of the greatest all-around men," but she likes sex with others:

I have had numerous sexual affairs, most of which are common knowledge to my husband but he doesn't mind as long as they're just physical and not emotional. In addition, we both have been into swinging for about a year, but swing only privately (although we tried group sex and didn't like it) with couples we both like and have other things in common with. We belong to a swingers' club where we meet hundreds of other couples, most of whom are married.

In contrast to the wives who enjoy swinging for the sexual variety and pleasure are those who think swinging will solve marital problems, or who go along because their husbands persuade them to do it. One wife, who at twenty-four has six children (ages ten, eight, six, three, two, and one), wonders why she gets "terribly uptight about life, sex, and everything in general," and why her married life is "such a real drag sometimes." She and her husband are thinking of swinging with some friends of theirs, which she hopes will dissipate her marital blahs without losing her husband's trust and support. "I don't want to end our marriage," she wrote, "but I feel sometimes it would do us good to have swinging affairs." For at least one wife who tried swapping to save her marriage, there was an unanticipated result:

I was married 11 years and had 3 children. I'm now separated, in the process of divorce, and have been living with another man whom I will marry when the divorce is final. Sex was totally unsatisfactory with my former husband and he threw me into a "swapping" situation. The one I swapped with is the one I intend to marry! I discovered with him that I am not frigid and now at age 34 I am finally fulfilled sexually.

The types and consequences of swinging are not much different from the types and consequences of other extramarital liaisons. Sociologist Brian Gilmartin documents the range of categories: "At one extreme are the purely sexual swingers who desire no social or emotional relationships with their partners. At the other extreme are the swingers who seek close and lasting relationships or friendships. In between are the 'recreational swingers,' who generally belong to swinging clubs with stable and limited memberships, and who consider the social aspects of swinging nearly as important as the sexual." As for effects, swinging seems beneficial for a good number of these couples, and it may shatter the already tenuous bonds between others.

Gilmartin interviewed 100 middle-class, married, suburban swinging couples in 1971, and matched them with 100 couples who were socioeconomically comparable but not swingers.* He found that swinging had little impact on the participants' marriages or on their marital sex lives. In fact, not one couple felt their marriage had become worse since they started swinging. Indeed, the swingers were happier with their marriages than the conventionally adulterous spouses among the matched couples. Gilmartin thinks that the open agreement between swinging spouses, and the shared ideology that sexual variety is desirable and healthy, accounts for this difference. "Normal" adultery, he says, is more prevalent in this society, but it is also more secretive. Adulterers usually don't have the moral support provided by a group.

A SUMMARY OF THE EXTRAMARITAL SCENE

Of all the women who participated in the *Redbook* survey, fewer than one in three have had a lover since marriage. Although most of the women who have affairs do so because of lack in the marriage—sexual problems, communication problems—some are able to balance lover and husband with relatively little conflict, often for several years. These women are as selective after marriage as they were before; only a small minority have more than five lovers, either premaritally or extramaritally.

The *Redbook* women are remarkably pragmatic, if we may read

---

*The differences between the two groups were few but interesting: The swingers tended to describe their childhoods as less happy than the controls did; swingers were less close to their parents; swingers were sexually and socially precocious and had married earlier. Both groups had grown up with the same ties to religion, but the swingers dropped their religious affiliations in adulthood. But on several tests of personal adjustment, the swingers and the matched controls did not differ; neither group was more neurotic or maladjusted than the other.

It should be kept in mind, however, that Gilmartin was interviewing swinging couples who were not especially representative of *all* couples who may have tried the experience. He got the regulars, not those who might have split up because one partner was unhappy.

between the numbers for a moment, about sex and marriage. Of the women who have extramarital affairs, most have had a casual, short-lived relationship rather than a romantic, consuming passion, and their experiences generally do not affect their relationship with their husbands. Of the monogamous wives, 62 percent said they *never* had a desire for an extramarital affair. But slightly less than half said they thought an outside relationship would never happen, although few are seeking one. When asked about the probability of a future extramarital affair, only 4 percent said it would definitely happen, only 9 percent said it would probably happen, and 38 percent said it might happen. They are leaving the door open, but not running through it like hounds to the hunt.

Most of these women want to be monogamous; those who foresee affairs for themselves feel deep problems at home.

> I have been fantasizing about having an affair for over a year now—I feel the reality of an affair is very near. If the decision presents itself—I don't know what I'll do. I am not happy with my marriage (11 years) and sadly do not anticipate a change for the better. Many discussions [with my husband] have led nowhere. He spends many hours in his business and I resent the many hours and feel deep hurt because of the many disappointments. It is hard for me to accept his view, that he is spending all this time and energy for *us,* for our future, for our children's future. I fear that when he is ready for us, it will be too late. All that we had and shared emotionally at one time is gone. Someday we will have so many wonderful expensive *things,* which is real nice, but it won't matter then. My heart truly aches for my children—they love him so intensely—but he has no time to listen, to look, to play. Why can't he see it now before it's too late?

This predicament is typical of many couples who reach different stages in their lives and have incompatible needs and goals. Some therapists used to assume that this incompatibility was due to unmeshed personalities, but now, as we learn more about conflicts over the entire life cycle, people are realizing that spouses change over the years of a marriage, but not necessarily at the same rate. The issues that matter to a wife in her twenties, when her energies are typically devoted to home and young children, subside when the wife hits her mid-thirties and her children are launched. Now she turns for redefinition and moral support to her husband, who is typically off on a career spiral and can't be bothered with wifely or household worries. Many women suspect that there is something wrong with *them,* or some fatal flaw in their marriages, if they are not in harmony with their husbands. It is hard to see the ways in which the structural demands of job, family, and housework influence the priorities of each spouse.

Enter extramarital sex, which may not solve problems but can make a person forget them for a while. It is not an inconsistency to say that the great majority of *Redbook* women love their husbands and are sexually satisfied at home, but that some also have a lover or two on the side—especially when they reach the critical age during the late thirties. Indeed, if you look through recent commentaries and studies of extramarital sex, you will observe a shift in the tone of the writings: Sex outside marriage, once thought to doom the family unit, is now regarded as having positive as well as negative effects. For example, Lonny Myers, a physician, and the Reverend Hunter Leggitt concluded from their interviews that extramarital sex occurs in both "good" and "bad" marriages, and that it is not predictably destructive. "We suspect most affairs are of such complex nature," they observe wisely, "that whether the net result is helpful or harmful remains an enigma even to the participants." They rattle off a stack of benefits that extramarital sex may impart: It lessens feelings of resentment that marriage is keeping one from experience or happiness; it makes a person feel alive, renewed, warm, attractive—all of which can benefit the spouse; it provides respite from marital and professional problems; it makes an unpleasant marriage tolerable, if the spouses don't want to divorce because of religion, children, or finances.

Mind you, Myers and Leggitt were not recommending that everyone should take a lover, along with a Vitamin C tablet, for daily health. They were not denying that extramarital sex can disrupt, even destroy, a marriage. They were simply trying to point out what so many of the *Redbook* women indicated: that there are many motives for extramarital sex, not all of them bad.

Whether to have an extramarital affair is a personal decision influenced by many things, most of which still elude researchers. As Bell and his colleagues observed, a wife's negative rating of her marriage was a better predictor than any demographic factor such as her age, education, or home town. But, they added, many women in happy marriages have extramarital sex, and many women in unhappy marriages do not. Obviously other forces are afoot, or abed. Most researchers agree, for instance, that as the strength of religious taboos declines, the rate of adultery should rise.

When Emma Bovary succumbed to temptation, she was, in the manner of romantic novels, transformed:

> But when she looked at her face in the glass she was surprised by what she saw. Never had her eyes looked so large, so black, so fathomless. Some subtle influence, diffused about her person, had transfigured her.

Most of the women in the *Redbook* study who had had an extramarital affair were not so transformed; they enjoyed their dalliances because they were, in the candid word of that happy wife, fun. But one forty-two-year-old newly remarried wife had this to say about her affair:

> I married my first husband because I was so hungry for a man to hold me close, to kiss me passionately, to hold my hand —silly things that teenagers do—and everything went along fine for the first 15 years of my marriage. My husband went his way, I went mine, it was my "duty" to make him sexually happy. I thought I had gotten over missing the love that should go with a happy marriage and sexual life, when, suddenly, when I was 34, it seemed that someone pulled a rope and jerked me awake. I looked inside myself and saw an empty shell, I was dead inside, all my feelings were lying there smoldering.

In this realization, and in her subsequent reawakening with a lover, she discovered Madame Bovary's truth:

She kept on saying to herself: "I have a lover—a lover!" finding joy in the thought, the joy of girlhood renewed as when she had for the first time realized the claims of her body. So, after all, she was to know the happiness of love! of those fevered moments of delight which she had despaired of finding. She stood on the threshold of a magic land where passion, ecstasy, delirium would reign supreme. A blue immensity was round her: the peaks of sentiment glittered for her in imagination. Mere ordinary existence seemed a thing far off and tiny, glimpsed far below in the shadows cast by those high immensities.

And that is what sexual passion, in or out of marriage, is all about. Love, ecstasy, and flight—however brief, however exquisite —from ordinary existence.

OLD NEWS AND NEW NEWS

Old News	*New News*
1. About the same number of wives are having extramarital sex now as in Kinsey's era . . .	1. . . . but they are starting earlier in their marriages.
2. Most wives who have extramarital sex are dissatisfied or bored with their marriages . . .	2. . . . but a substantial minority happily enjoy their husbands *and* their lovers.
3. Women who have extramarital sex are not having more partners than they ever did (still very few) . . .	3. . . . but they tend to have a casual dalliance rather than a long-lasting love affair.
4. Women anticipate more guilt . . .	4. . . . than they usually feel.
5. Religious devoutness still acts to inhibit extramarital sex . . .	5. . . . but religious devoutness tends to decline with age, length of marriage, and the opportunity for an affair.
6. The double standard still lives in people's attitudes . . .	6. . . . but men and women are behaving in more similar ways.
7. The great majority of American wives are monogamous and would like to stay that way.	7. The great majority of American wives are monogamous and would like to stay that way.

5
THE GOOD NEWS ABOUT MEN
by Carol Tavris

The elephant, the huge old beast,
  is slow to mate;
he finds a female, they show no haste,
  they wait

for the sympathy in their vast shy hearts
  slowly, slowly to rouse
as they loiter along the river-beds
  and drink and browse

and dash in panic the brake
  of forest with the herd,
and sleep in massive silence, and wake
  together, without a word.

So slowly the great hot elephant hearts
  grow full of desire,
and the great beasts mate in secret at last,
  hiding their fire.

Oldest they are and the wisest of beasts
  so they know at last
how to wait for the loneliest of feasts,
  for the full repast.

They do not snatch, they do not tear;
  their massive blood

> moves as the moon-tides, near, more near
> till they touch in flood.
>   —D. H. LAWRENCE
>   "The elephant is slow to mate"

> *Higgamous, hoggamous, women monogamous,*
> *Hoggamous, higgamous, men are polygamous.*
>   —ANONYMOUS

For, once you get down to it, you find there are no similarities between men and women, aside from avarice, lust, and sloth.
                  —Columnist in L.A. *Times*

This book has been as much about men as about women. The *Redbook* survey did not give husbands the chance to speak up in their own behalf (or, occasionally, in self-defense), but the happiness and sexual satisfaction of their wives reflects well on them. They may take a bow.

The 100,000 silent husbands in this study are an invisible testimonial to the strength of the sexual bond between women and men. The bond is buffeted daily, however, by the media blitz on the female half, which comes dangerously close to obscuring a simple truth. As the *Redbook* survey showed, for the vast majority of people in this country, sexual happiness rests on warm communication and trust between the sexes, not on the sexual agility and technique of one. So I couldn't leave this book without a word about the overlooked sex, the newly defensive sex: men.

The first thing to observe about the stronger sex is that they aren't. Men are no less vulnerable than women to the insecurities of the sexual game, and they are as easily intimidated. In a 1976 article for *New York* magazine on similarities between the sexes ("Good News About Sex"), I observed that men were fortunate to have been spared the Freudian legacy of worrying whether one's orgasms were "mature" and "correct." Women had long endured the physiologically absurd distinction between vaginal and clitoral orgasms, I said, but men never had to wonder whether they were having, say, a mature "hilt" orgasm instead of a childish "head" variety.

A friend of mine read this section of the essay and stopped dead, as if hit by a wet blasphemy. "Did Masters and Johnson find out about that distinction?" he asked, staring at me nervously.

I stared back. "But I made that up," I said. "You *can't* believe I was serious. Surely you recognize the deft sarcasm?"

He blushed, but didn't back down. "Well, I knew just what you meant by hilt versus head," he mumbled. "I've had both kinds."

You see what a precarious situation we've gotten into. If people are that ready to dive headlong into categories, one must tread the sexual waters carefully. I think the first order of business, actually, is to get men and women into the same category. This is not easy to do, because we all have been weaned on *vive la différence* theories about the sexes, and our beliefs about the opposing natures of men and women are embedded like grit in our language and observations. "Men are just big demanding babies," a wife will say. "Women are overemotional adolescents," a husband will say. We get these generalizations from long experience, part pleasurable, part painful, and no one wants to part with a cherished bias without a fight.

Naturally, men and women are not exactly alike in their sexual behavior and attitudes. Their experiences and opportunities tend to be different in childhood and adolescence—it's a rare girl who joins in group masturbation, for example, but "circle jerks" are not uncommon among boys. Many girls learn to use sex to get love, while many boys pretend love to get sex. The sexual worries that girls report include fear of pregnancy, fears about their reputation, concern about not reaching orgasm, anxiety about attractiveness; the main worry that boys have about sex is how to get more of it. And as for adults, wives are still wishing that their husbands were more communicative, emotionally expressive, and verbal in their lovemaking; the men want different sorts of communication. Husbands don't feel loving until their wives act sexy, therapists say. Wives don't feel sexy until their husbands act loving. In the languages of marriage, much is often lost in the translation.

The trouble is that many people assume that the different styles of men and women, which seem so basic, are the result of genetically programmed differences in sexuality. "Look here," said my neighbor to a visiting sexologist, "what is so much talk and research going to accomplish? Sex is just a matter of instinct, after all." "Instinct, schminstinct," the expert replied, rather concisely, I thought. "There's not one thing natural about nature."

In fact, human beings have sexual urges and desires, just as they get hungry for food. But how to act on those hungers, with whom, under what conditions, following which rules, when, and how often are all culturally learned. For example, many societies and religions regulate the frequency of intercourse. Orthodox Jewish women are not to have intercourse during menstruation and for seven days thereafter. Among the Etoro tribe, heterosexual intercourse is taboo for up to 260 days a year. Catholic nuns and priests, and other religious groups, take a vow of chastity. But nowhere has it been observed that people die of celibacy as they die of starvation.

The main argument against the notion of biological differences in sex drive between men and women is that it doesn't sit still. American society has regarded the male as having the stronger sex drive—poor creatures, slaves to the urgent pleading of the penis. But in other ages and cultures women were considered the voracious sex, so full of throbbing impulses that they had to be chained with prohibitions so that men could get on with the business of civilization. In New Britain, reports anthropologist Gayle Rubin, "men's fear of sex is so extreme that rape appears to be feared by men rather than women. Women run after the men, who flee from them, women are the sexual aggressors, and it is bridegrooms who are reluctant." "Just like the girls at Columbia," says a young male student I know.

His candid observation points out that the pendulum is swinging back again. Partly because of the publicity about the female's capacity for multiple orgasms, the new mythology says that women are the sexier sex. Psychoanalyst Mary Jane Sherfey, extrapolating from Masters and Johnson's data, goes so far as to offer the assurance that "the human female is sexually insatiable in the presence of the highest degrees of sexual satiation." (So there, fellas.) Merely one generation ago, people were equally convinced that males were the insatiable ones. In 1943, a gynecologist asserted that the male, designed to fertilize as many human flowers as he could lay hand on, "has an infinite appetite and capacity for intercourse." One writer believes in female sexual primacy, the other in male sexual primacy; but actually both would agree that the sexes are fundamentally different.

The research on human sexuality persuades me, however, that we can drop this zigzag, who's-on-top game for good. Most of the sexual differences between men and women are culturally, not biologically, created and perpetuated. That, when you think about it, is good news—because if the sexes stopped hurling biological inevitabilities at each other, they could stop counting orgasms and sex acts and begin to revel in the sweet similarities of rhythm and response.

Let us consider the evidence behind some of the more popular assumptions about male and female sexuality:

1. *Orgasms are different for women and men, in quantity and quality.*

When Alfred Kinsey reported that a small proportion of the women he interviewed (14 percent) could have a series of orgasms in a single session, his news was greeted with disbelief and derision. Two male psychiatrists immediately wrote a book to argue that Kinsey had been taken in by frigid females or nymphomaniacs who wouldn't know an orgasm from a stomachache. A decade later, in the mid-sixties, Masters and Johnson told us—in the midst of throwing words like "frigid" and "nymphomaniac" out the window—that the multiple orgasm was within the potential of any woman, and that with continued stimulation women could have as many climaxes as a gothic novel.

But the researchers did not make headlines with another major observation, namely that the female orgasm and the male orgasm were more alike than different. In both sexes, the main consequence of sexual arousal is vasocongestion of the genital area; blood flows into the organs and tissues and distends them. The skin flushes, the heart pounds, breathing gets heavy. The orgasm itself is precisely analogous in both sexes: Contractions occur rhythmically about every eight tenths of a second. The first few of these contractions are the most intense, and may be followed by several irregular and less-intense ones. New research, as experimental psychologist Linda Rosen reports, even shows that orgasm produces profound changes in brain-wave patterns in both sexes, literally an altered state of consciousness. Orgasm does make you lose your mind.

Recently I found an ingeniously simple study that demonstrates beautifully the *subjective* similarities between male and female orgasm. Males are supposed to have sudden, violent, explosive orgasms, centered in the genitals, while females experience undulating waves of sensation, distributed throughout the body. Right? Think again. Three researchers, E. B. Proctor, N. Wagner, and Julius Butler, asked men and women to write down descriptions of how orgasm felt to them (they discarded the people who didn't know). Proctor and her colleagues changed only those words that revealed the sex of the author; for example, "penis" was changed to "genitals" and "husband" to "spouse." Then they gave the forty-eight descriptions to a panel of seventy judges, men and women who were gynecologists, clinical psychologists, and medical students. The experts had merely to indicate which sex wrote each description.

They couldn't do it. Most of them got about 50 percent right, no better than chance guesses. In describing what orgasm felt like, both males and females wrote about "a build-up of tension which starts to pulsate very fast," "intense excitement of [the] entire body," "a tightening inside, palpitating rhythm, explosion and warmth and peace." And both sexes waxed positively lyrical: "An orgasm feels like heaven in the heat of hell"; "it's like jumping into a cool swimming pool after hours of sweating turmoil"; "it's like shooting junk on a sunny day in a big, green, open field." I was as unsuccessful as the experts in judging which sex had written which description; we have all been too influenced, I guess, by D. H. Lawrence and Henry Miller. (If you think you're so good at telling the difference, try your hand with the eight descriptions that follow.)

Which of the following descriptions of orgasm were written by women, and which by men?

1. For me, orgasm feels like a building wave of emotion. First I notice a pulsing sensation that is quite localized, then it spreads through my whole body. Afterwards, I feel tired but also super-relaxed.   W_x__ M____

2. Sexual orgasm just seems to happen to me. I can't explain how or why, but I suddenly experience an intense rush of

feeling, and then it's gone, just as suddenly. Often, I want to experience it more than once.   W_____ M_×_

3. Just before orgasm, I am mostly aware of the muscle contractions. When the orgasm comes, I feel my whole body sort of explode, and then slip into a deep relaxation, so that I feel I can hardly move.   W_×_ M_____

4. My anxiety about sex definitely inhibits my orgasm. There are times that I feel some intense sensations, but usually I am too inhibited to really let myself go. If I am not very comfortable with my partner, it is very difficult to come. I have orgasms most easily when I masturbate.   W_____ M_×_

5. Basically, I feel a glow which starts in my genitals, and then spreads through my whole body. Sometimes one orgasm is enough, and other times it is not completely satisfying.   W_×_ M_____

6. I think orgasm is overrated. I sometimes spend over an hour getting turned on, and then the orgasm takes only a few seconds. I'd like to learn how to make the feeling of orgasm last longer.   W_____ M_×_

7. I concentrate all my attention on the sensations in the genitals, and when I come, I completely lose contact with everything around me. My body feels incredibly alive, and seems to vibrate. Afterwards, I just want to hold my lover and be very still.   W_×_ M_____

8. Just before I reach orgasm, I feel warmth in my genital area. The warmth turns into a heat which spreads up my back, and all the way into my fingers and toes. Although I am usually fairly quiet during most of lovemaking, at orgasm I often moan quite loudly.   W_____ M_____

Answers: M 'W 'W 'W 'W 'W 'W 'W

The only orgasmic difference between men and women, Masters and Johnson reported, occurs after the first orgasm. Women, if properly stimulated, can continue to have climaxes, while men enter a refractory period, during which they cannot have another erection no matter what they do or what anyone does to them. Now researchers are rethinking even this basic discrepancy. Some women have multiples, sure, but others say they have orgasms "like a man's"—a final whammo orgasm that leaves them exhausted and insensitive to further touch. Everyone I talk to has her own name for it. The knockout. The volcano. The submarine (little orgasms that zip along under the surface and finally emerge). The firecracker.

And at last, belatedly, sexologists report what men ought to have been asserting all along: The male orgasm is not so boring and predictable after all. Some men have climaxes "like a woman's"—a series of orgasms that vary in intensity and quantity. Yes, quantity. Not all males immediately enter a long refractory period after ejaculation: some can have several orgasms in a row at fifteen- to sixty-second intervals. I had always assumed that for men, orgasm and ejaculation go together like bagels and lox—one isn't much good without the other. But the two processes are distinct. Males can reach a climax without ejaculating, and this is true for adults as well as for young boys who are not yet physiologically mature.

Finally, some attention to the men! Drs. Mina Robbins and Gordon Jensen were among the first researchers to bring the male multiple orgasm into the laboratory and watch it in action. They began with one young man who said that he often had repeated orgasms without ejaculation prior to his final, most intense orgasm with ejaculation. These five or six "preliminary" orgasms, he said, lasted a minute each. So Robbins and Jensen observed him make love to his female companion, while he was wired for sight, sound, and response. Their machines recorded all the signs of sequential orgasms: increased respiration and heart rate, muscular tension, urethral and anal contractions, and the altered states of consciousness that accompany orgasm. After each orgasm the man's erection lessened slightly for fifteen or twenty seconds, and then the next buildup to another orgasm began.

What one man can do, Robbins and Jensen reasoned, lies in reach of others. And they found others. Fourteen additional men, age twenty-five to fifty-five, merrily demonstrated their capacity for multiple orgasms. One man, age forty-nine, decided to see how far he could go and how much control he could muster over the number of pre-ejaculatory orgasms. He got to twenty-five before going over the final cliff, Jensen told me in the calm tones of a man for whom the remarkable has become mundane. "Twenty-five?" I gulped, striving for a professional tone of detachment. "That's not so many," he replied. "They're only a minute each."

The aim of all this research, though, is not to set new performance standards for either sex, but to show what babies we are when it comes to understanding sexual potential and how similar male and female potentials are. If we impose artificial boundaries on our responsiveness, if we set up false distinctions between male sexuality and female sexuality, we create self-fulfilling prophecies. The truth is that individuals have a wide range of physical reactions during sex, from gentle ripples to full-fledged Hollywood fits. But people prefer to extrapolate from individual differences to gender differences. In an informal poll of my friends on the question "Which sex is noisier during lovemaking?" I got roaring disagreement. Some said that men were more controlled and silent. "It's a built-in genetic trait," said my friend the anthropologist, "from having to be alert for saber-toothed tigers and jealous husbands." Some insisted that women were quieter, more inhibited (a built-in trait, no doubt, from having to be alert for crying infants and jealous wives). Once the cultural veneer is peeled off, and our preconceptions compared with our real experiences, I think we'll find few built-in differences in orgasmic response.

2. *Men turn on faster than women do; they are quick to become aroused, while women take a slow climb to excitement.*

"Oh yeah," the reader is probably thinking at this point, "there sure is one built-in difference. A man turns on like a shot, but some women take hours." Men complain that women need too much foreplay; women complain that men are too eager to dispense with preliminaries and dash into the main event.

But even this sex difference is learned, not instinctive. As noted in Chapter Three, when women masturbate they are aroused as rapidly as men are. And in many cultures men learn how to control the speed of arousal, for the increased pleasure of both partners. The Hindu practice of Karezza, the Oneida commune's practice of ejaculatory control, the Mangaian male's custom of delaying orgasm until the female has had several orgasms—all testify to the extent to which male response can be controlled. In societies like ours, where many males have their early sexual experiences under conditions of high stress and pressure for speed —the back seats of cars, the imminent arrival of parents at home, the time constraints with prostitutes—sexual responses become conditioned accordingly. After a while, speedy turn-ons and speedier ejaculations seem inevitable and biologically normal. But what is inevitable in one culture is barbaric in another and what is learned can be unlearned. Today, as the *Redbook* survey suggests, men and women may not be operating at sexually different speeds, as they once did. As each woman learns the habits of her own body and recognizes what best excites her, as each man learns that there is more to sexual response than ejaculation, couples should stop singing those old different-rhythm blues.

3. *Men are more aroused by pornography than women and have different sexual fantasies, further evidence of the male's greater sex drive.*

Kinsey found a major sex difference in the way men and women responded to pornographic films and books. Generally speaking, men responded and women didn't. The trouble with determining whether this result reflected a "natural" difference between men and women—say, that men are simply more excited by external stimuli—was that women were under heavy cultural pressure to be repelled by erotic material. Nor did they have equal opportunity to get hold of pornography, which was, and is, more acceptable in masculine circles. For that matter, pornography has long been created by and for the male sex.

Researchers since Kinsey find that equality makes itself felt in this area as in others. Gunter Schmidt and Volkmar Sigusch, two West German sex researchers, have been studying responses to pornography for several years, and they find that sex differences in arousability are strongly related to "the grade of sexual emancipation of women in a society." West German students, they point out, are quite a bit more emancipated than Americans of Kinsey's generation, and possibly more than their American counterparts today. In a recent study, they showed erotic films and slides to 128 males and 128 females, on themes ranging from masturbation to coitus, with petting, fellatio, and cunnilingus along the way. Then they asked the students what they thought about the films and whether they were aroused by them. According to their self-reports, 86 percent of the men reacted physiologically (with moderate to strong erections) and so did 72 percent of the women (with vaginal lubrication and sensations). The men tended to say they enjoyed the pornography more than the women did, but the difference between them was not pronounced—there were many individual reactions. As Schmidt and Sigusch reported, "42 percent of the women regarded the slides or films [as] more arousing than did the average man."

Apparently the young are becoming emancipated in this country too. Psychologist Julia Heiman asked her students to listen to different sorts of taped stories, some highly erotic, some romantically loving but not sexually explicit, some both romantic and explicit. For both sexes it took the direct juicy descriptions, with or without the roses and moonlight, to turn people on. Women were just as aroused by the stories as the men were, although the popular assumption is that women prefer soft fade-outs to direct hard-ons. Indeed, the *Redbook* women suggest how much things have changed since Kinsey's study. As we noted, about 60 percent of them have been to a pornographic movie and occasionally use erotic books or films for sexual arousal and foreplay. It will be interesting to see how women are affected by erotic films made by and for themselves.

The sexual-fantasy gap between the sexes seems to be closing, too. We used to hear provocative tales about women's fantasies about being raped, and some therapists and laymen were persuaded that such fantasies meant that women were sexual masochists, desiring that the dream come true. Some women actually got to worrying whether their occasional image of being overtaken by Robert Redford meant they really wanted to be pawed by sweaty strangers in a dark alley. Then a few thoughtful researchers dragged the rape-fantasy issue out of its psychoanalytic lair and did a few studies with healthy women rather than neurotic patients. E. Barbara Hariton, for example, interviewed 141 housewives about their fantasies during intercourse. "The study showed that erotic fantasies are common among women, that they are not escape mechanisms, and that they often enhance sexual pleasure and desire," she wrote. Moreover, the women who had occasional fantasies of being overpowered by a man were the most self-confident, independent, and sexually satisfied.

As usual, no one was asking the men about their fantasies; male fantasies were as uninteresting to people as male orgasms. Last year I prepared a survey on masculinity for *Psychology Today* magazine, and I sneaked in a few questions to test my hunch that men, like women, occasionally dream of being ravished by the opposite sex. I was right. Of the 28,000 replies from men and women, half of both sexes said they have rape fantasies every so often, though only 3 percent of the men and 7 percent of the women said they have such fantasies often. There it is. In this time of sexual uncertainty, when the rules of conduct shift on social quicksand, both sexes indulge in the comfortable dream of sex without responsibility, guilt, worry about performance, or fuss. I somehow doubt, though, that a hue and cry will be raised about men's natural masochistic tendencies and how they really want hordes of insatiable females to attack them. Or even one insatiable female.

Just when men are beginning to acknowledge that they too have the traditional female fantasy of playing the passive role, playing the desirable partner whose sexiness overcomes Sophia Loren or Raquel Welch, now women are writing about the traditional male fantasy: fast, assertive, erotic encounters without emotional entanglements. In fact, some of the new women writers scare men in the brutal candor of their sexual descriptions. Erica Jong's Isadora seeks sex without physical barriers, such as zippers and girdles, or emotional ones, such as feelings of guilt. Gael Greene's Kate describes the male anatomy as clinically and dispassionately as Henry Miller did the female's. Francine du Plessix Gray's Stephanie calls the sexual shots, and her young men whine for more emotional and intellectual commitment. If anyone thinks that female writers are shyer, more cautious, or more circumspect in their sexual writings than men, they should hie themselves down to their local bookshop. Recent books by women are as explicitly erotic as any that men have written.

My argument is not a moral or evaluative one, I should add. I am not saying that pornography, ravishment fantasies, or sexy books are good or bad. That is a matter of personal and sexual preference. My point is simply that women are not "naturally" sweeter, more moral, more masochistic, or less sexually motivated than men. When the barriers that divide men's roles from women's roles break down, it turns out that women can be just as nice or nasty as men, and certainly just as sexy. And men, when freed from the strong-and-silent constraints of the masculine role, confess that their feelings are not so different from women's.

Ross Wetzsteon, reflecting on the aggressive quest of modern women for sexual liberation through impersonal encounters, describes his own experience of being regarded as a sex object: "The horrible thing about being treated as a collection of parts is that parts are easily replaceable. If a woman regards you as a sex object, it's frighteningly easy for her to transfer her passion to another man." Indeed, *fear, terror, fright* punctuate Wetzsteon's article like gunshot. "By its very nature sexuality contains a certain element of terror," he writes. When sex is depersonalized, "it touches the tenderest core of our anxieties about sexual identity":

> We're never more alone, and yet never closer to another person, than at the moment of orgasm. And to treat people as sex objects is to deny the fulfillment this paradox promises, the fulfillment you can't achieve in a solipsistic erotic frenzy, the fulfillment you can feel only in the simultaneous sense of surrender to self and union with another.

Shades of what women have been saying for decades.

I think what we are seeing in society these days is not a polarization of the sexes or a reversal of sex roles, but a greater expression by men *and* women of the range of sexual behavior and fantasy. Both sexes have the same erotic passions. Both have the same insecurities and worries. Both occasionally want to lie back and enjoy it, and both occasionally want to grab it aggressively with both hands. For both, sex with love is better than sex without. Well, whaddaya know?

4. *Men and women reach their "sexual peaks" at different stages in the life cycle: Males peak in their teens, females not until their thirties. Women wear well, men wear out.*

If this one were true, the best marriages would be between seventeen-year-old boys and thirty-five-year-old women. Both, according to sex researchers, are at the peak of sexual potency and responsiveness. Both are at their insatiable best.

Sex therapists Helen Singer Kaplan and Clifford Sager, in summarizing the course of sexual response for each sex, describe the difference between the average man and woman. Males hit their orgasmic heights in their late teens, when they are literally sex-obsessed. They cannot get enough. Throughout their twenties, they act on this urgency, often to the puzzlement or despair of their wives or girlfriends, who do not share their insatiability. Young men have erections easily (sometimes *too* easily, they will admit in embarrassment, as on buses or in libraries), and detumescence after orgasm is slow. In their thirties, men are satisfied with fewer orgasms and less preoccupied with sexual fantasies; the refractory period between orgasms begins to lengthen, to up to one half hour by the late thirties. In their forties, men find their sexual pleasure changing in quality; orgasm becomes less important than the total sensual experience. Among men in their fifties and sixties, the sexual drive continues to diminish, though men still have erection and orgasm. Some men, however, may be so absorbed in their careers that they can go for weeks without a sexual thought or impulse.

If men begin their sexual histories at a gallop and end with a walk, the assumption goes, women begin at a crawl and end at a gallop. Adolescent girls are less interested than boys in sex for orgasmic release, and it takes them longer to learn about their own orgasmic potential. As we noted, a fairly high proportion of the *Redbook* women were nonorgasmic before marriage, and the proportion who have frequent orgasms increases with the length of marriage. By their mid-thirties, women reach their maximum responsiveness, and, once turned on, they don't turn off. Now it is the women who want sex more often than their husbands; it is at this age that wives are most likely to have extramarital affairs. Women remain capable of all sexual activity well into old age, though their desire may diminish. "In terms of frequency," Kaplan and Sager observe, "an 80-year-old woman apparently has the same physical potential for orgasm as she did at 20!"

The life cycles of male and female sexuality certainly sound terribly determined by biology, some impish trick of nature to keep the sexes apart. But a description of what happens *on the average* is not the same as proving that what happens to many people must happen to all. Many people used to die by age thirty, too, but there was nothing biologically programmed about it. Description is not causality. Sexual behavior is a result of many factors. Some are physical, such as the state of the central nervous system, hormone levels, general health, and energy. Some are psychological, such as learned patterns of sexual response, inhibitions and guilts, conflicts and desires, conditioned fantasies. Some are environmental, such as the sexual ambience of the society, its sexual values and taboos. It is too simple to reduce male–female differences to biology.

The belief that sexual peaks are governed by physiological imperatives sets up expectations about normalcy, which in turn affect what people do and think they can do. If men expect their performance to decline, they are not surprised if it happens, and their expectation may contribute to the decline. They may even welcome the excuse. But there are many social reasons for male mid-life sexual lag: boredom, work pressures or the peak of career achievement, lack of sexual excitement, a stagnant marriage, personal insecurities, and fears about the future. Similarly, there are many social reasons for the longer time it takes women to reach their sexual stride. The evidence that women hit their peak in their thirties, remember, came from generations of women who spent their teens inhibiting themselves and their twenties trying to shake those inhibitions. The women I know who learned about their own anatomy and sexual capabilities when they were teenagers did not wait any fifteen years to blossom.

As the double standard dies, we will be able to see better which of the heralded differences in sexual peaks come from culture and which from biology. I think we will be pleasantly surprised. Many people have good and satisfying sex lives well into old age, as the letters from numerous *Redbook* respondents testified. Male potency does not inevitably decline, and some men even keep the fascinating ability to have multiple orgasms. A healthy man, as Kaplan and Sager note, "is able to enjoy sexual intercourse throughout life. Indeed, freed of the intense need for fast orgastic release and the inhibitions of his youth, more satisfying and imaginative love play is often enjoyed by the older man." Ironically, and happily, life-cycle changes can bring the sexes closer together, rather than isolating them: Love and sensuality become more important to men once they have lost the sexual urgency of adolescence; sexual expression becomes more important to women once they have lost the diffuse romanticism of adolescence and learned about their bodies. The two sexes meet in mid-life.

It is as reasonable a scenario as any other. But if people "know" that the male orgasm is a one-shot affair and that male performance must decline with age, it won't occur to either sex that men too can learn to expand their sexual responsiveness. Frank Beach, an eminent psychologist, cites an example of an anthropologist who was used to having sex once a week at home. On a field trip, however, he "found it expedient to meet the daily demands of a native woman. Though it took some time to get used to the new rhythm, within a few months he found himself as happy with the daily schedule as he had been with the weekly one. When the field trip was over, he readjusted (with some difficulty) to his original frequency." The "daily demands" of the woman, incidentally, were themselves influenced by culture, for in some places she would have been considered normal and in others a nymphomaniac.

But my favorite bit of evidence for the flexibility of so-called sexual peaks comes from a family reunion, where I witnessed an exchange between my cousin Mark, age twenty-eight, and my cousin Claire, age thirty-two. "You look gorgeous," he said to her, "and very sexy. You must be in love. Who is he?" She described him in detail. He prodded for more information, and then asked her lover's age. "In his fifties," she said. "Ah, I see," he said gently. "So yours is an affair of the heart and head. After all, how could a man that age satisfy a woman in her prime?"

I loved her catlike smile as much as her answer. "Mark," she said, "you have a lot to look forward to."

Everything considered, the good news about men is that they aren't all that different from women. The sooner that men and women recognize that their sexual needs and capabilities are closer than they thought, the better their relationships will be. Communication is the key to pleasure. And for the majority of our *Redbook* women, their husbands are listening.

APPENDIX

Questionnaire and Responses

Percentage of respondents precedes each choice.
An asterisk (*) indicates questions for which women could give multiple answers. Some demographic items have been eliminated from the following list, e.g., race of respondent and respondent's spouse (virtually all were Caucasian).

1. How would you characterize your general feelings over the past few months?
   - 56.8% A. Happy most of the time.
   - 19.1% B. Sometimes happy.
   - 17.0% C. Sometimes unhappy.
   - 6.6% D. Mostly unhappy.
2. In general, how would you rate your marriage at this time?
   - 44.9% A. Very good.
   - 35.9% B. Good.
   - 13.7% C. Fair.
   - 4.5% D. Poor.
   - 1.1% E. Very poor.
3. In general, how would you evaluate the sexual aspect of your marriage?
   - 32.8% A. Very good.
   - 34.2% B. Good.
   - 21.0% C. Fair.
   - 8.5% D. Poor.
   - 3.4% E. Very poor.
4. Thinking back over the past few months, what was the average number of times you had sexual relations with your husband each month?

  1.6% A. None.

26.4% B. 1 to 5 times.

31.7% C. 6 to 10 times.

20.7% D. 11 to 15 times.

11.3% E. 16 to 20 times.

  8.3% F. 21 or more times.

5. As to the frequency of intercourse in your marriage, would you say it is . . .

57.6% A. About right?

  4.3% B. Too frequent?

38.1% C. Too infrequent?

6. Do you achieve orgasm . . .

15.0% A. All the time?

48.2% B. Most of the time?

19.1% C. Sometimes?

10.6% D. Once in a while?

  7.0% E. Never?

7. On the average, about how long must foreplay last for you to become sexually aroused?

29.0% A. 1 to 5 minutes.

43.3% B. 6 to 10 minutes.

19.6% C. 11 to 15 minutes.

  5.4% D. 16 to 20 minutes.

  1.2% E. 21 to 25 minutes.

  1.6% F. 26 minutes or more.

8. On the average, how long must sexual intercourse last for you to have an orgasm?

28.0% A. 1 to 5 minutes.

37.0% B. 6 to 10 minutes.

20.1% C. 11 to 15 minutes.

  9.0% D. 16 to 20 minutes.

  2.8% E. 21 to 25 minutes.

  3.1% F. 26 minutes or more.

9. Do you think there are specific times most appropriate for sex?

35.8% A. Yes, certain times are most appropriate.

64.2% B. No, any time is appropriate.

*10. If yes, what do you think are the most appropriate times for sex?

16.1% A. In the morning.

71.0% B. At night.

12.0% C. On weekends.

  0.9% D. On certain established days of the week.

11. Do you think there are specific places most appropriate for sex?

56.5% A. Yes, certain places are most appropriate.

43.5% B. No, any place is appropriate.

*12. If yes, what do you think are the most appropriate places for sex?

47.3% A. In the bedroom.

44.2% B. Anywhere in the home.

8.5% C. Other.

13. In the sex act, do you play an active part?

37.1% A. Always.

38.5% B. Usually.

11.4% C. About half the time.

11.9% D. Sometimes.

1.1% E. Never.

14. Do you like to dress in sexually erotic clothing as a stimulus to lovemaking?

65.7% A. Yes.

34.3% B. No.

*15. If yes, what kinds of clothing do you like to wear when you wish to appear sexually erotic?

40.0% A. Lingerie or lacy, feminine clothing.

20.1% B. Low-cut, black or obviously suggestive clothing.

6.7% C. Whatever is casual and comfortable.

3.5% D. Fashionable, current styles.

27.7% E. I prefer to be naked.

2.0% F. Other.

16. Do you ever vary the locations or settings for sex to make it more exciting?

76.2% A. Yes.

23.8% B. No.

*17. If yes, what change of setting do you prefer?

49.1% A. Some room in the house other than the bedroom.

22.7% B. Hotel or motel.

18.5% C. Outdoors.

9.7% D. Other.

18. How often would you say you initiate sex?

1.5% A. Always.

9.1% B. Usually.

43.8% C. About half the time.

41.9% D. Sometimes.

3.7% E. Never.

*19. How do you let your partner know you are interested in sex?

54.0% A. Caress or cuddle him.

31.9% B. Tell him.

37.8% C. Touch his genitals.

13.6% D. Flirt.

18.0% E. He just knows.

2.7% F. Other.

20. Do you ever use any devices for sexual stimulation in your love-making?

    21.0% A. Yes.

    79.0% B. No.

*21. If yes, what are the devices you use?

    38.5% A. Vibrator.

    18.8% B. Penis-shaped objects.

    24.9% C. Oils.

    2.0% D. Feathers.

    15.8% E. Other.

22. If yes, is the use of these devices pleasurable?

    56.9% A. Yes, always.

    40.2% B. Yes, sometimes.

    2.9% C. No.

23. Have you ever seen a pornographic movie?

    60.5% A. Yes.

    39.5% B. No.

*24. If yes, whom were you with?

    76.1% A. Husband.

    7.3% B. Lover.

    7.7% C. Male friend.

    6.3% D. Female friend.

    2.6% E. Other.

25. Have you ever used erotic movies, books or pictures as a part of sexual arousal or foreplay?

    3.2% A. Often.

    42.9% B. Occasionally.

    9.5% C. Once.

    44.5% D. Never.

26. Has your husband ever performed oral-genital sex (cunnilingus) on you?

    38.8% A. Often.

    47.9% B. Occasionally.

    6.0% C. Once.

    7.3% D. Never.

27. How would you describe this experience?

    62.4% A. Very enjoyable.

    28.3% B. Somewhat enjoyable.

    4.2% C. No particular feelings about it.

3.6% D. Unpleasant.
1.5% E. Repulsive.
28. Have you ever performed oral-genital sex (fellatio) on your husband?
40.2% A. Often.
44.8% B. Occasionally.
5.9% C. Once.
9.1% D. Never.
29. How would you describe this experience?
34.1% A. Very enjoyable.
38.3% B. Somewhat enjoyable.
13.0% C. No particular feelings about it.
12.1% D. Unpleasant.
2.5% E. Repulsive.
30. Has your husband ever performed anal intercourse with you?
1.6% A. Often.
18.7% B. Occasionally.
22.3% C. Once.
57.3% D. Never.
31. How would you describe this experience?
9.6% A. Very enjoyable.
30.8% B. Somewhat enjoyable.
10.2% C. No particular feelings about it.
41.9% D. Unpleasant.
7.5% E. Repulsive.
32. Have you ever, since the age of 18, had a sexual experience with another woman?
0.4% A. Often.
0.8% B. Occasionally.
1.7% C. Once.
97.2% D. Never.
33. How would you describe this experience?
35.2% A. Very enjoyable.
35.2% B. Somewhat enjoyable.
16.7% C. No particular feelings about it.
13.0% D. Unpleasant.
0.0% E. Repulsive.
34. Have you ever masturbated since your marriage?
15.7% A. Often.
51.6% B. Occasionally.
6.7% C. Once.
26.1% D. Never.
35. Would you describe this as a sexually satisfying experience?

31.4% A. Yes, always.

49.0% B. Yes, sometimes.

19.6% C. No.

*36. If you have masturbated since your marriage, for what reasons or under what circumstances have you usually done so?

37.9% A. My husband has been absent.

18.0% B. Coitus has not been satisfying.

8.6% C. My husband has found it sexually stimulating to watch.

31.0% D. It has been an enjoyable sexual experience quite apart from intercourse.

15.6% E. I have used it as a means of sexual experimentation.

31.0% F. I have used it as a way of relaxing tensions.

14.1% G. It is a habit I developed before marriage.

6.9% H. Other.

37. Have you ever had sexual relations while under the influence of alcohol?

12.5% A. Often.

69.9% B. Occasionally.

7.3% C. Once.

10.3% D. Never.

38. Has the use of alcohol contributed to a good sexual experience?

38.4% A. Yes.

43.0% B. Sometimes.

18.6% C. No.

39. Have you ever had sexual relations while under the influence of marijuana?

5.2% A. Often.

9.3% B. Occasionally.

6.0% C. Once.

79.4% D. Never.

40. Has the use of marijuana contributed to a good sexual experience?

62.7% A. Yes.

16.2% B. Sometimes.

21.1% C. No.

41. Did you have sexual intercourse before you were married?

80.7% A. Yes.

19.3% B. No.

42. If yes, how old were you the first time?

13.1% A. 15 years old or under.

35.5% B. 16 to 17 years old.

32.6% C. 18 to 19 years old.

12.4% D. 20 to 21 years old.

6.4% E. Over 21 years old.

43. With how many men did you have premarital intercourse?

51.4% A. 1 man.

33.5% B. 2 to 5 men.

8.8% C. 6 to 10 men.

6.4% D. More than 10 men.

44. In your premarital sexual experience, about how many times did you have intercourse with each partner?

8.2% A. Once.

27.6% B. 2 to 5 times.

9.6% C. 6 to 10 times.

54.6% D. More than 10 times.

45. In your premarital sexual experience, how often did you reach orgasm?

6.7% A. All the time.

22.6% B. Most of the time.

36.5% C. Sometimes.

34.2% D. Never.

46. Would you object to a son's having premarital intercourse?

13.9% A. Yes.

46.5% B. No.

39.5% C. I don't know.

47. Would you object to a daughter's having premarital intercourse?

25.1% A. Yes.

33.3% B. No.

41.6% C. I don't know.

48. Since your marriage, have you ever had sexual relations with a man other than your husband?

29.1% A. Yes.

70.9% B. No.

49. If yes, with how many different men?

50.5% A. 1 man.

39.7% B. 2 to 5 men.

4.9% C. 6 to 10 men.

4.9% D. More than 10 men.

50. What was the approximate number of times you had sexual relations with each man?

6.1% A. Once.

20.4% B. 2 to 5 times.

7.1% C. 6 to 10 times.

40.2% D. More than 10 times.

26.2% E. It varied greatly from partner to partner.

51. Did your extramarital partner ever perform oral sex (cunnilingus) on you?

17.7% A. Often.

27.7% B. Occasionally.

15.4% C. Once.

39.2% D. Never.

52. Did you ever perform oral sex (fellatio) on him?

16.8% A. Often.

27.6% B. Occasionally.

15.5% C. Once.

40.2% D. Never.

53. If you have never had an extramarital sexual experience, have you ever had a fairly strong desire to do so?

37.8% A. Yes.

62.2% B. No.

54. What would you say is the probability that you will have an extramarital sexual experience in the future?

48.8% A. It will never happen.

38.2% B. It might happen.

8.7% C. It will probably happen.

4.3% D. It will definitely happen.

55. Have you ever engaged in mate swapping, where you and your husband exchanged partners with another couple for the purpose of having sexual relations?

0.6% A. Often.

1.2% B. Occasionally.

1.9% C. Once.

96.3% D. Never.

56. If you have not engaged in mate swapping, would you like to do so at some time in the future?

1.6% A. Yes.

4.9% B. Perhaps.

17.4% C. I'm not sure.

76.1% D. Definitely not.

57. Do you discuss intimate sexual feelings and desires with your husband?

21.3% A. Always.

25.6% B. Often.

44.8% C. Occasionally.

8.4% D. Never.

*58. Do you discuss intimate sexual feelings and desires with people other than your husband?
   42.0% A. Yes, with female friends.
   8.7% B. Yes, with male friends.
   13.3% C. Yes, with mother, sister or female relative.
   12.2% D. Yes, with lover.
   7.7% E. Yes, with professional, such as therapist or counselor.
   4.0% F. Yes, with others.
   38.9% G. I never discuss these feelings.

*59. Of all aspects of sexual activity, which one do you like the best?
   31.1% A. Everything.
   19.6% B. Intercourse.
   23.1% C. Orgasm.
   16.9% D. Foreplay.
   3.6% E. Masturbation.
   10.2% F. Oral Sex.
   0.7% G. Anal sex.
   20.8% H. Satisfying my partner.
   40.3% I. Feeling of closeness with my partner.

*60. Of all aspects of sexual activity, which one do you like the least?
   15.5% A. There is nothing I dislike.
   17.8% B. Messiness after intercourse.
   5.8% C. Oral sex.
   27.4% D. Anal sex.
   19.1% E. Not reaching orgasm.
   23.6% F. Routine or boring sex.
   3.2% G. Other.

61. What is your age?
   2.6% A. Under 20.
   23.4% B. 20 to 24.
   32.1% C. 25 to 29.
   19.8% D. 30 to 34.
   9.1% E. 35 to 39.
   13.0% F. 40 or over.

62. How long have you been married?
   5.0% A. Less than a year.
   29.4% B. 1 to 4 years.
   21.5% C. 5 to 7 years.
   11.9% D. 8 to 10 years.
   32.2% E. More than 10 years.

63. How many children do you have?

21.5% A. None.
22.9% B. One.
29.8% C. Two.
14.9% D. Three.
 5.9% E. Four.
 5.0% F. Five or more.
*64. How old are your children?
11.8% A. Under 1 year.
41.5% B. 1 to 5 years.
29.0% C. 6 to 11 years.
18.2% D. 12 to 17 years.
12.6% E. 18 years or over.
 65. What is your religious affiliation?
56.9% A. Protestant.
27.2% B. Catholic.
 3.2% C. Jewish.
 5.9% D. Agnostic.
 6.8% E. Other.
 66. Would you describe yourself as . . .
11.0% A. Strongly religious?
40.0% B. Fairly religious?
33.2% C. Mildly religious?
15.9% D. Not religious?
 67. How would you describe your political views?
 3.9% A. Very liberal.
22.9% B. Liberal.
56.6% C. Moderate.
14.6% D. Conservative.
 2.1% E. Very conservative.
 68. What is the highest level of education you have completed?
 1.2% A. Grade school.
37.4% B. High school.
37.7% C. Some college.
13.3% D. College graduate.
 6.9% E. Some graduate school.
 3.6% F. Advanced degree.
 69. What is the approximate annual income of your family?
 1.7% A. Less than $5,000.
 8.5% B. $5,000 to $7,999.
 9.3% C. $8,000 to $9,999.
21.0% D. $10,000 to $12,999.
15.0% E. $13,000 to $14,999.

32.6% F. $15,000 to $24,999.

12.0% G. $25,000 or more.

70. Are you presently working for pay outside the home?

    32.0% A. Yes, I have a full-time job (30 or more hours a week).

    16.7% B. Yes, I have a part-time job (less than 30 hours a week).

    10.6% C. No, I do volunteer work.

    40.7% D. No.

71. If you are presently employed, what is your occupation?

    1.5% A. Professional with advanced degree (for example, doctor, lawyer).

    22.2% B. Teacher, counselor, social worker, nurse.

    12.4% C. Managerial, administrative, business.

    44.9% D. White-collar (sales, clerical, secretarial).

    1.8% E. Artist, writer.

    0.1% F. Farming, agriculture.

    4.5% G. Technician, skilled worker.

    5.2% H. Semiskilled or unskilled worker.

    1.1% I. Student.

    6.4% J. Other.

72. If you are not working now but were employed before marriage, what was your occupation?

    0.8% A. Professional with advanced degree (for example, doctor, lawyer).

    16.3% B. Teacher, counselor, social worker, nurse.

    7.3% C. Managerial, administrative, business.

    47.3% D. White-collar (sales, clerical, secretarial).

    0.3% E. Artist, writer.

    0.3% F. Farming, agriculture.

    4.9% G. Technician, skilled worker.

    7.7% H. Semiskilled or unskilled worker.

    9.7% I. Student.

    5.5% J. Other.

73. If you are married, what is your husband's occupation?

    10.0% A. Professional with advanced degree (for example, doctor, lawyer).

    6.6% B. Teacher, counselor, social worker, nurse.

    27.7% C. Managerial, administrative, business.

    7.0% D. White-collar (sales, clerical, secretarial).

    1.0% E. Artist, writer.

    3.7% F. Farming, agriculture.

23.3% G. Technician, skilled worker.

9.2% H. Semiskilled or unskilled worker.

1.8% I. Student.

9.6% J. Other.

74. Do you live in a . . .

   22.0% A. Big city (one with a population of at least 500,000)?

   27.3% B. Small city?

   21.2% C. Suburb?

   19.7% D. Small town?

   9.7% E. Farm area?

75. Where do you live?

   8.5% A. New England.

   19.3% B. Mid-Atlantic states.

   9.6% C. South-Atlantic states.

   25.0% D. North-central states.

   14.7% E. South-central or Southwest states.

   4.4% F. Mountain states.

   6.5% G. West Coast, north.

   8.4% H. West Coast, south.

   0.4% I. Alaska or Hawaii.

   3.7% J. Other.

BIBLIOGRAPHY

Athanasiou, Robert. A review of public attitudes on sexual issues. In Joseph Zubin and John Money (Eds.), *Contemporary Sexual Behavior: Critical Issues in the 1970s*. Baltimore: The Johns Hopkins University Press, 1973, 361–390.

_____. Phillip Shaver, and Carol Tavris. Sex. *Psychology Today*, July 1970, *4*, 39–52.

Bartell, Gilbert. *Group Sex*. New York: New American Library, 1971.

Bauman, Karl. Volunteer bias in a study of sexual knowledge, attitudes, and behavior. *Journal of Marriage and the Family*, 1973, *35*, 27–31.

Beach, Frank. It's all in your mind. *Psychology Today*, July 1969, *3*, 33–35, 60.

Bell, Robert R., and P. L. Bell. Sexual satisfaction among married women. *Medical Aspects of Human Sexuality*, December 1972, *6*, 136–144.

_____. and Jay B. Chaskes. Premarital sexual experiences among coeds, 1958 and 1968. *Journal of Marriage and the Family*, 1970, *32*, 81–84.

_____. and Dorthyann Peltz. Extramarital sex among women. *Medical Aspects of Human Sexuality*, March 1974, *8*, 10 ff.

_____. Stanley Turner, and Lawrence Rosen. A multivariate analysis of female extramarital coitus. *Journal of Marriage and the Family*, 1975, *37*, 375–384.

Belliveau, Fred, and Lin Richter. *Understanding Human Sexual Inadequacy.* New York: Bantam, 1970.

Bernard, Jessie. *The Future of Marriage.* New York: Bantam, 1973.

Brecher, Edward M. *The Sex Researchers.* Boston: Little, Brown, 1969.

Campbell, Angus. The American way of mating: marriage sí, children only maybe. *Psychology Today,* May 1975, *8,* 37–44.

Christensen, Harold T., and Christina F. Gregg. Changing sex norms in America and Scandinavia. *Journal of Marriage and the Family,* 1970, *32,* 616–627.

Clark, Alexander L., and Paul Wallin. Women's sexual responsiveness and the duration and quality of their marriages. In Nathaniel N. Wagner (Ed.), *Perspectives on Human Sexuality.* New York: Behavioral Publications, Inc., 1974, 178–199.

Cox, Harvey. Evangelical ethics and the ideal of chastity. *Christianity and Crisis,* April 27, 1964, *24,* 75–80.

Croake, James W., and Barbara James. A four-year comparison of premarital sexual attitudes. *The Journal of Sex Research,* 1973, *9,* 91–96.

Cuber, John F. The natural history of sex in marriage. *Medical Aspects of Human Sexuality.* July 1975, *9,* 51 ff.

————. Sex in five types of marriage. In Leonard Gross (Ed.), *Sexual Issues in Marriage.* Holliswood, N.Y.: Spectrum Publications, Inc., 1975, 3–16.

Davis, Keith. Sex on the campus: Is there a revolution? *Medical Aspects of Human Sexuality,* 1971, *5,* 128–142.

DeBurger, James E. Sex in troubled marriages. *Sexual Behavior,* May 1972, *2,* 22–26.

Framo, James L. How does an affair affect a marriage? In Leonard Gross (Ed.), *Sexual Issues in Marriage.* Holliswood, N.Y.: Spectrum Publications, Inc., 1975, 187–198.

Gagnon, John H. *Human Sexualities.* Glenview, Ill.: Scott, Foresman and Co., 1977.

Gebhard, Paul H. Factors in marital orgasm. *Journal of Social Issues,* 1966, *22,* 88–95.

Gilmartin, Brian. That swinging couple down the block. *Psychology Today,* February 1975, *8,* 54–58.

Glenn, Norval D. The contribution of marriage to the psychological well-being of males and females. *Journal of Marriage and the Family,* 1975, *37,* 594–601.

Grabill, Wilson H. Premarital fertility. *Current Population Reports,* U.S. Department of Commerce Bureau of the Census, August 1976.

Gross, Leonard (Ed.). *Sexual Issues in Marriage.* Holliswood, N.Y.: Spectrum Publications, Inc., 1975.

Hariton, E. Barbara. The sexual fantasies of women. *Psychology Today,* March 1973, *6,* 39–44.

Heiman, Julia R. The physiology of erotica: Women's sexual arousal. *Psychology Today,* April 1975, *8,* 90–94.

Hite, Shere. *The Hite Report.* New York: Macmillan, 1976.

Hunt, Morton. *The Affair.* New York: World Publishing, 1969.

_____. *Sexual Behavior in the 1970's.* New York: Dell Publishing Co., 1974.

Jessor, Shirley, and Richard Jessor. Transition from virginity to nonvirginity among youth: A social psychological study over time. *Developmental Psychology,* 1975, *11,* 473–484.

Johnson, Ralph E. Attitudes toward extramarital relationships. *Medical Aspects of Human Sexuality,* April 1972, *6,* 168 ff.

Kaats, Gilbert, and Keith Davis. Effects of volunteer biases in studies of sexual behavior and attitudes. *Journal of Sex Research,* 1971, *7,* 219–227.

Kantner, John F., and Melvin Zelnik. Sexual experience of young unmarried women in the U.S. *Family Planning Perspectives,* 1972, *4,* 9–18.

Kaplan, Helen S. *The New Sex Therapy.* New York: Quadrangle/The New York Times Book Co., 1974.

_____, and Clifford J. Sager. Sexual patterns at different ages. *Medical Aspects of Human Sexuality,* June 1971, *5,* 10 ff.

Kinsey, Alfred C., Wardell B. Pomeroy, Clyde E. Martin, and Paul H. Gebhard. *Sexual Behavior in the Human Female.* New York: Pocket Books, Inc., 1965.

Krafft-Ebing, Richard von. *Psychopathia Sexualis.* New York: G. P. Putnam's Sons, 1965.

Levinger, George. Husbands' and wives' estimates of coital frequency. *Medical Aspects of Human Sexuality,* September 1970, *4,* 45–57.

Levitt, Eugene E., and Albert D. Klassen. Public attitudes toward sexual behavior: The latest investigation of the Institute for Sex Research. Paper presented at the American Ortho-psychiatric Association Convention, 1973.

Marshall, Donald S., and Robert C. Suggs (Eds.). *Human Sexual Behavior: The Range and Diversity of Human Sexual Experience Throughout the World.* New York: Basic Books, 1971.

Maslow, A., and J. M. Sakoda. Volunteer-error in the Kinsey study. *Journal of Abnormal and Social Psychology,* 1952, *47,* 259–267.

Masters, William H., and Virginia E. Johnson. *Human Sexual Response.* Boston: Little, Brown, 1966.

————. *Human Sexual Inadequacy.* Boston: Little, Brown, 1970.

McDermott, Sandra. *Female Sexuality: Its Nature and Conflicts.* New York: Simon & Schuster, 1970.

Mead, Beverley T. What impact does adultery generally have on a marriage? *Medical Aspects of Human Sexuality,* October 1975, *9,* 122 ff.

Moore, Kristin A., and Steven B. Caldwell. The decline in age at first intercourse among adolescent females in the United States. Unpublished manuscript, the Urban Institute, Washington, D.C., 1977.

Myers, Lonny, and Hunter Leggitt. A new view of adultery. In Leonard Gross (Ed.), *Sexual Issues in Marriage.* Holliswood, N.Y.: Spectrum Publications, Inc., 1975, 165–186.

Neubeck, Gerhard. Roundtable: The significance of extramarital sex relations. *Medical Aspects of Human Sexuality,* October 1969, *3,* 33 ff.

Newman, Gustave, and Claude R. Nichols. Sexual activities and attitudes in older persons. In Nathaniel N. Wagner (Ed.), *Perspectives on Human Sexuality.* New York: Behavioral Publications, Inc., 1974, 501–508.

Ogren, David. Sexual guilt, behavior, attitudes, and information. Unpublished dissertation, University of Houston, 1974.

Peplau, Letitia Anne, Zick Rubin, and Charles T. Hill. Sexual intimacy in dating relationships. *Journal of Social Issues,* in press, 1977.

Pfeiffer, Eric. Sex and aging. In Leonard Gross (Ed.), *Sexual Issues in Marriage*. Holliswood, N.Y.: Spectrum Publications, Inc., 1975, 43–48.

Pomeroy, Wardell B. *Dr. Kinsey and the Institute for Sex Research*. New York: Harper & Row, 1972.

Proctor, E. B., N. N. Wagner, and Julius C. Butler. The differentiation of male and female orgasm: an experimental study. In Nathaniel N. Wagner (Ed.), *Perspectives on Human Sexuality*. New York: Behavioral Publications, Inc., 1974, 115–132.

Reiss, Ira L. *Premarital Sexual Standards in America*. Glencoe, Ill.: The Free Press, 1960.

———. Premarital sexual standards. In Carlfred B. Broderick and Jessie Bernard (Eds.), *The Individual, Sex, and Society*. Baltimore: The Johns Hopkins University Press, 1969, 109–118.

———. The influence of contraceptive knowledge on premarital sexuality. *Medical Aspects of Human Sexuality*, February 1970, *4*, 71 ff.

Rosen, Linda. The experience of orgasm: His and hers. *Advisor: The Journal of Human Sexuality*, April 1977, *II*, 30–35.

Rubin, Gayle. The traffic in women. In Rayna R. Reiter (Ed.), *Toward an Anthropology of Women*. New York: Monthly Review Press, 1975, 157–211.

Rubin, Isadore. *Sexual Life after Sixty*. New York: Basic Books, 1965.

Salzman, Leon. Female infidelity. *Medical Aspects of Human Sexuality*, February 1972, *6*, 118 ff.

Schmidt, Gunter, and Volkmar Sigusch. Sex differences in responses to psychosexual stimulation by films and slides. In Nathaniel N. Wagner (Ed.), *Perspectives on Human Sexuality*. New York: Behavioral Publications, Inc., 1974, 96–114.

Shaver, Phillip, and Jonathan Freedman. Your pursuit of happiness. *Psychology Today*, August 1976, *10*, 26–32, 75.

Sherfey, Mary Jane. *The Nature and Evolution of Female Sexuality*. New York: Random House, 1972.

Smith, Leon. Some trends in religion's response to the new sexuality. "New Perspectives on Human Sexuality," The Milton S. Eisenhower Symposium 1974. The Johns Hopkins University, November 6, 1974.

Sontag, Susan. The double standard of aging. *Saturday Review,* September 23, 1972, 29–38.

Sorensen, Robert C. *Adolescent Sexuality in Contemporary America.* New York: World Publishing, 1973.

Sorg, David A., and Margaret B. Sorg. Sexual satisfaction in maturing women. *Medical Aspects of Human Sexuality,* February 1975, *9,* 62 ff.

Tavris, Carol. Good news about sex. *New York,* December 6, 1976, *9,* 51–57.

―――. Men and women report their views on masculinity. *Psychology Today,* January 1977, *10,* 35–42, 82.

Terman, Lewis M. *Psychological Factors in Marital Happiness.* New York: McGraw-Hill, 1938.

Thurber, James, and E. B. White. *Is Sex Necessary?* New York: Harper & Row, 1957.

Tiefer, Leonore. Bargaining in bed: "I won't say you're a lousy lover if you make me feel loved" and other trade-offs. *Ms.,* November 1976, *5,* 77–80.

Udry, J. Richard, Karl E. Bauman, and Naomi M. Morris. Changes in premarital coital experience of recent decade-of-birth cohorts of urban American women. *Journal of Marriage and the Family,* 1975, *37,* 783–787.

Vener, Arthur M., and Cyrus S. Stewart. Adolescent sexual behavior in middle America revisited: 1970–1973. *Journal of Marriage and the Family,* 1974, *36,* 728–735.

Wagner, Nathaniel N. (Ed.). *Perspectives on Human Sexuality.* New York: Behavioral Publications, Inc., 1974.

Weinberg, Martin S. (Ed.). *Sex Research: Studies from the Kinsey Institute.* New York: Oxford University Press, 1976.

Westoff, Charles F. Coital frequency and contraception. *Family Planning Perspectives,* 1974, *6,* 136–142.

Wetzsteon, Ross. Do men want to be sex objects? *Village Voice,* November 1, 1976, 11–13.

Wolfe, Linda. *Playing Around: Women and Extramarital Sex.* New York: New American Library, 1975.

Zelnik, Melvin, and John F. Kantner. Sexual and contraceptive experience of young unmarried women in the United States, 1976 and 1971. *Family Planning Perspectives,* March/April 1977, *9,* 55–71.

———. The probability of premarital intercourse. *Social Science Research,* 1972, *1,* 335–341.

INDEX

Abortion, 57
Active role, 80–82
Acton, William, 4–5
Affair, The (Hunt), 124–125
Affairs, extramarital, 4, 55, 165–166
  adjusting to, 131
  and age, 55
  benefits, 139
  degree of involvement, 127
  frequency of sex, 165–166
  and guilt, 142
  length of, 142
  number experiencing, 114, 142
  number of lovers, 165
  reasons for, 122–127, 129, 130–132,
    137–138
  and religion, 142
Age
  and eroticism, 70–73
  and happiness, 63
  at sexual initiation, 43–49
  and mate-swapping, 135
  and oral sex, 87
  and orgasm, 156
  and premarital sex, 164–165
  of respondents to questionnaire, 21
  and sex drive, 155–158
  and sexual satisfaction, 105–106
Alcohol, and sex, 84, 164
Anal sex, 4, 83, 90–94, 103, 163
  and age, 94
  and extramarital sex, 116, 124
  percent experiencing, 93

Arousal
  male-female differences, 151–152
  and pornography, 152–153
  time needed, 77, 78
Attentiveness, of husbands, 131–132
Awakening, The (Chopin), 112

Bartell, Gilbert, 134–135
Baumann, Karl, 14
Beach, Frank, 158
Behn, Aphra, 27
Bell, Robert, 17, 36, 115, 122, 125,
    129, 140
Bell Jar, The (Plath), 28
Bernard, Jesse, 61
Bias, and sex studies, 13–14, 17
Birth control. *See* specific methods
Bolling, David, 92
Boredom
  and affairs, 125, 142
  and swinging, 136
Boys, sexual worries of, 145. *See also*
    Teenagers
Butler, Julius, 148

Caldwell, Steven, 57, 58
Campbell, Angus, 62
Catholics, 21, 38, 39, 40, 146

Catholic Theological Society of America, 101
Chaskes, Jay, 36
Chastity, 146
Childbirth, and sex, 85–86
Children
  effect on parents' sex life, 84–85
  parents' sexual attitude, 165
  parents' view of premarital sex, 51
  of respondents, 23
Chopin, Kate, 32, 112
Christianity and Crisis (Cox), 43
Church, effect on sex, 38. *See also* Religion
Clothing, erotic, 83
Colette, 61
College women, 35–36
Commission on Population Growth and the American Future, 36
Communication, sexual, 24–25, 106–110, 166–167
  percent discussing sex, 107
Comparison, sexual, 4–10
Contraceptives, 56–58
Cox, Harvey, 43, 102
Croake, James, 33, 35
Cuber, John, 72
Cunnilingus, 4, 6, 79, 83, 86, 87, 88, 89, 118, 166
Customs, sexual, 146

Davis, Keith, 14
De Vries, Peter, 111–112, 113
Different Woman, A (Howard), 113
Dildos, 83
Disraeli, Benjamin, 61
Donne, John, 1
Double standard, 59, 115, 142
Drive, sex, 41, 68, 146
  measuring, 10–12
Du Plessix Gray, Francine, 154

Educational Ministries in Marriage, 101
Education
  and oral sex, 87

Education (Cont.)
  and premarital sex, 45–46
  of respondents, 22
  and sex, 102
Employment
  and extramarital sex, 126–127
  of respondents, 22
  and sex, 64
Environmental factors, and sexual behavior, 157
Erotic films, 152–153
Eroticism, and age, 70–73
Excitement, and extramarital affairs, 133

Fantasies, sexual, 152–155
Fear of discovery, and affairs, 128
Fear of Flying (Jong), 119, 120
Fears, of sexual initiation, 28–29
Fellatio, 4, 82, 83, 86, 87, 88, 89, 118, 166
Female sexuality, 4–7
Fidelity, 8
Fifteen-year-olds, 46–47, 48, 49, 59
Flaubert, Gustave, 112
Ford, Betty, 29
Foreplay, 76, 77, 79
  length of, 160
Freedman, Jonathan, 100
Frigidity, 74, 78
Functions and Disorders of the Reproductive Organs (Acton), 4–5

Gagnon, John, 116
Geographic area, of respondents, 21
Gilmartin, Brian, 136–137
Girls, sexual worries of, 145. *See also* Fifteen-year-olds; Teenagers
Going All the Way (Wakefield), 33
Golden Notebook, The (Lessing), 54
Greene, Gael, 154
Group, The (McCarthy), 31, 52
Group sex, 134
Group Sex (Bartell), 134–135
Guilt, 50–51, 53, 97, 102
  and affairs, 127–128, 142

Happiness
and frequency of sex, 66–67
and marriage, 62–63, 64
researching, 64–65
Hariton, E. Barbara, 153
Hazlitt, William, 64
Heiman, Julia, 153
Hill, Charles, 36
Hite, Shere, 16–17, 19, 94
Hite Report, 78
Homosexuality, 48, 63–64, 163
Howard, Jane, 113
Hunt, Morton, 15, 19, 37, 47, 74, 77,
87, 115, 116, 124, 135
Husbands, communication with, 106–
110. *See also* Marriage

Illegitimacy, 57
Impotence, 71
Income, of respondents, 22
Incompatibility, 138–139
Institute of Sex Research, 29
Intercourse, sexual
active role, 161
clothing preference, 161
first, 3–4, 59
frequency, 66–70, 159–160
initiating, 80–82, 161–162
length of, 160
premarital, 3, 29–30, 32, 42, 164–
165
and confidence, 58
and education, 43
and marriage, 54–56, 59
in 1960s, 36
in 1970s, 36
number of lovers, 46, 48
percent experiencing, 34, 59
variety, 33
specific places for, 160–161
specific times for, 160
Is Sex Necessary? (Thurber and
White), 25–26
IUD, (intrauterine device) 58

James, Barbara, 33
Jensen, Gordon, 92, 150–151

Jessor, Richard, 36
Jessor, Shirley, 36
Jews, 21, 38, 39, 40, 146
Johnson, Virginia E. *See* Masters and
Johnson
Jong, Erica, 119, 120, 154

Kaats, Gilbert, 14
Kantner, John, 29, 36, 37, 44, 57
Kaplan, Helen Singer, 156, 157
Key Clubs, 134
Kinsey, Alfred C., 12–13, 14, 15, 19,
34, 38, 39, 42, 43, 44, 45, 47, 51,
52, 53, 54, 64, 68, 74, 75, 76, 86,
91, 97–98, 114, 115, 116*n.*, 117,
142, 147, 152, 153
Klassen, Albert, 29, 114
Krafft-Ebing, Richard von, 86

Lady Chatterley's Lover (Lawrence),
42, 90
Last Tango in Paris, 92
Lawrence, D. H., 90, 143–144, 148
Leggitt, Rev. Hunter, 139
Lessing, Doris, 54
Levitt, Eugene, 29, 114
Life cycles
male-female, 157–158
and marriage, 138–139
Liquor. *See* Alcohol
Love, and sex, 31, 34, 115, 124, 158
extramarital, 130
Lovemaking, The (Merriam), 60
Lovers. *See also* Affairs
number of, 46, 48, 49, 118
Lutherans, 101

Madame Bovary (Flaubert), 112, 140–
141, 144–148
Male-female differences, 144–148
Male sexuality, 7–8
Marijuana, and sex, 84, 164
Marriage, 61–62
complaints, 68–69

Marriage (Cont.)
  effect of swinging on, 137
  and extramarital sex, 122, 125
  length of
    and orgasm, 74, 75, 76
    and sex, 63, 67–68
  and premarital sex, 37, 38, 45
  rating, 159
    and extramarital sex, 122
  successful, and affairs, 129, 130
  unsuccessful, 7–9
Maslow, Abraham, 13–14
Masters and Johnson research, 11*n.*, 42, 71, 146, 147, 149–150
Masochism, 153, 154
Masturbation, 47, 48, 52, 94–95, 123, 151, 163–164
  frequency, 96
Mate-swapping, 134–137, 166
Mayhew, Henry, 61
McCarthy, Mary, 31, 52
Measurement, by questionnaire, 10–25
Medical Aspects of Human Sexuality, 92
Men, vulnerability of, 144. *See also* Male-female differences
Menopause, and sex, 71
Menstruation, 68
Merriam, Eve, 60
Method, research, 15–20
Methodists, 101
Miller, Henry, 148, 154
Monogamy, 113, 138, 142
Moore, Kristin, 57, 58
Morris, Naomi, 68
Multiple partners, and orgasm, 54
Myers, Lonny, 139

National Sex Forum, 101
Necking, 33
Neubardt, Selig, 92
Nin, Anaïs, 73
Nonorgasmic women. *See* Frigidity
Normality, 5–9
"Nuit Blanche" (Colette), 61

Office of Population Research, 66
Ogren, David, 97, 102

Opinion polls, 19
Oral-genital sex, 4, 78, 79, 83, 86–90, 98–99, 103, 108–109, 119, 162–163
Orgasm, 18, 51–53, 155
  and age, 53, 156
  and arousal, 73–80
  descriptions, 148–151
  difficulty reaching, 79–80
  and enjoyment, 75–76, 80
  females, 59
  frequency, 160
  love, 53
  male, 144–145
  male-female differences, 147–148
  methods of reaching, 78–79
  multiple, 147, 149, 150
  and oral-genital sex, 90
  percent reaching, 74
  and premarital sex, 165
  time reaching, 76–78

Parent, Gail, 42
Passive role, 80–82
Passivity, male, 154
Peplau, L. Anne, 36
Petting, 33
Physical factors, and sexual behavior, 157
Piercy, Marge, 35–36
Pills, contraceptive, and teenagers, 56–58
Plath, Sylvia, 28
Playboy, 87
Playboy Foundation, 15, 37–38
Playing Around (Wolfe), 119
Political views, of respondents, 22
Pomeroy, Wardell, 12–13
Pornography, 42, 83, 98, 152–155, 162
Premarital Sexual Standards (Reiss), 35
Privacy, 4–10
  and sex, 84–85
Proctor, E. B., 148
Promiscuity, 3, 47
Protestants, 21, 38, 39, 40
Psychological factors, 96–110
  and sexual behavior, 157
Psychology Today, 19, 100, 154

Psychopathia Sexualis (Krafft-Ebing), 86

Questionnaire
profile of respondents, 10–25, 167–170
and responses, 159–170
truthfulness of responses, 68

Rape fantasies, 153–154
Rationalization, and affairs, 128
Reiss, Ira, 35, 39, 50, 57
Religion, 53
and extramarital sex, 114–115, 117
and masturbation, 98
and oral sex, 87
and premarital sex, 38–41, 42, 43, 44
prohibitions, 97
of respondents, 21
and sex, 3
and sexual satisfaction, 97–106
Research
on happiness, 64
reliability of, 68
Respondents, types of, 12–15, 17, 19–23, 167–170
Rhythm method, 57
Robbins, Mina, 150
Roiphe, Anne, 29
Romanticism, 24
Rosen, Lawrence, 115, 125, 129
Rosen, Linda, 147
Rubin, Gayle, 146
Rubin, Zick, 36

Sager, Clifford, 156, 157
Sakoda, J. M., 13–14
Salzman, Leon, 120–121, 128
Satisfaction, sexual, 146. *See also* Orgasm
Schmidt, Gunter, 152–153
Self-esteem, and extramarital affairs, 124, 125–126
Sex frequency, and orgasm, 73

Sex objects, men as, 155
Sex-rating, 159
Sexual Behavior in the Human Female (Kinsey), 19. *See also* Kinsey
Sexual Behavior in the 1970's, 15
Sexual customs, 151–152
Sexual devices, 83, 98, 162
Sexual dissatisfaction, and extramarital affairs, 123–124
Sexual Freedom League, 134
Sexual peaks, 155–158
Sexual potential, 151
Sexual roles, changes in, 154
Shaver, Phillip, 100
Sheila Levine Is Dead and Living in New York (Parent), 42
Sherfey, Mary Jane, 146
Shelley, Percy Bysshe, 61
Sigusch, Volkmar, 152–153
Small Changes (Piercy), 35–36
Smith, Rev. Leon, 101
Social conditioning, 52
Sodomy. *See* Anal sex
Solomon, Neil, 29
Stewart, Cyrus, 37
Swingers, 134–137, 166
profile of, 135–137

Teenagers, 3–4, 29–30
and casual sex, 59
and the pill, 56–58
and premarital sex, 37, 44
sexual drive, 156
Thurber, James, 2, 25–26
Tiefer, Leonore, 24
Tropic of Cancer (Miller), 42
Turner, Stanley, 115, 125, 129

Udry, Richard, 68

Vener, Arthur, 37
Vibrators, 48, 83
Virginity, 28–29, 32–43
at marriage, 34

Wagner, N., 148
Wakefield, Dan, 33
Wetzsteon, Ross, 155
White, E. B., 2, 25–26
Wife-swapping, 134
Wilde, Oscar, 61

"Willing Mistress, The" (Behn), 27
Wolfe, Linda, 119

Zelnik, Melvin, 29, 36, 37, 44, 57